Explore the Everglades

TeakWood Press Geotravel Guides

Don't just visit a place, experience it with a TeakWood Press geotravel guide. Geotravel guides show you how to enrich your travels by understanding the places you go, the things you see and the people you meet.

- *Discover Natural South Florida: Nature Walks, Tours and Sites* (Available 1992)

- *Explore the Everglades*

Explore the Everglades

Miriam Lee Ownby

TeakWood Press
Kissimmee, Florida

Published by

TeakWood Press
160 Fiesta Drive
Kissimmee, Florida 34743
407-348-7330
Order Desk: 800-654-0403

Cover design by Paul LiCalsi, L&L Graphics
Interior illustrations by Jackie Magee

Printed in the United States of America

Library of Congress Cataloging-in-Publication Data
Ownby, Miriam Lee.
    Explore the everglades / Miriam Lee Ownby
        p.   cm.
    Includes index.
    ISBN 0-937281-06-9 : $9.95
        1. Everglades National Park (Fla.)--Guide-books.   2.
Everglades (Fla.)--Description and travel--Guide-books.   3.
Natural history--Florida--Everglades National Park--Guide-books.   4.   Natural   history--Florida--Everglades--Guide-books.   I. Title.
F317.E9096 1992   91-22935
917.59'390443--dc20   CIP

ISBN 0-937281-06-9 (pbk.)

Acknowledgements

The author wishes to make grateful acknowledgement:

To the personnel of Everglades National Park for their courteous help, especially Pat Tolle, Public Affairs Specialist for supplying information materials; to William B. Robertson, Jr., Research Biologist for discussing research findings and Allen Mebane, formerly Chief Naturalist for information about educational activities in the park.

To Cathy Anclade, Director of Communications for South Florida Water Management District for answering my questions and supplying numerous publications.

To Ruth Harley of the Institute for Children's Literature for encouragement and editorial assistance.

Contents

Maps

Illustrations

Introduction

South Florida's Everglades was once a fifty-mile-wide, six-inch-deep river flowing, almost imperceptibly, south and southwest from Lake Okeechobee to Florida Bay and the Gulf of Mexico. Writer and staunch Everglades defender Marjory Stoneman Douglas designated it "the river of grass." Its native inhabitants, the Seminole Indians, call it *Pa-Hay-Okee* — grassy waters.

Following decades of attempts to dry it up — and open the land to development and farming — the Everglades today remains only as remnants of the original river. About fifty percent of the Everglades has been altered to form Water Conservation Areas. Some thirty percent has been claimed for agriculture and development. Only about twenty percent has been preserved as Everglades National Park and Big Cypress National Preserve.

This alteration and fragmentation critically endangers the Everglades system. Everglades National Park, lying at the downstream end of the system, is especially vulnerable. To give you an idea of the damage done to the park, some estimates claim the population of wading birds has decreased as much as ninety-five percent since the 1930s. In spite of that sad statistic, when you visit you will find that thousands of birds still survive — at least for the present.

The Everglades is actually part of a larger system of creeks, streams, rivers and lakes known as the Kissimmee-Okeechobee-Everglades System. Its headwaters are located in Central Florida near Orlando and Disney World. In wet times, water from the Big Cypress Swamp located west of the Everglades augments the flow. The system terminates in Everglades National Park where the water flows into Florida Bay. This is the system I invite you to explore.

You can explore the system's elements as your time and interests dictate. This book exists to help you put each element into perspective as a part of the whole and to emphasize that the health of each element depends on the health of the whole.

As you read, please note that terms appearing in **bold italics** are listed and defined in a glossary at the back of the book. As you explore — even if only through the pages of this book — I hope you will come to appreciate the Everglades' uniqueness, special beauty and fragility and so will join with all who work to ensure its survival.

Be aware, in exploring, of South Florida's two seasons: a warm wet season from May to October and a cooler, drier season from November through April. You'll enjoy your explorations more during the drier winter season. The lower humidity and temperatures make walking the trails more comfortable and pleasant, and bothersome mosquitoes are less numerous. In addition, birds and animals concentrate at water holes in the dry season, so they become more available to visitors

Long-sleeved shirts and long pants will give protection from occasional pests. Comfortable walking shoes are important. If you are venturesome and your explorations call for getting your feet wet on a swamp — or "wet" — walk, bring a change of shoes. You'll also want to bring along some insect repellant. Sunscreen on any exposed skin is a wise precaution even in winter.

Binoculars can add to your pleasure in wildlife watching, and a camera lets you bring home tangible memories. Remember, though, to take only pictures and leave only footprints. And never feed the wildlife.

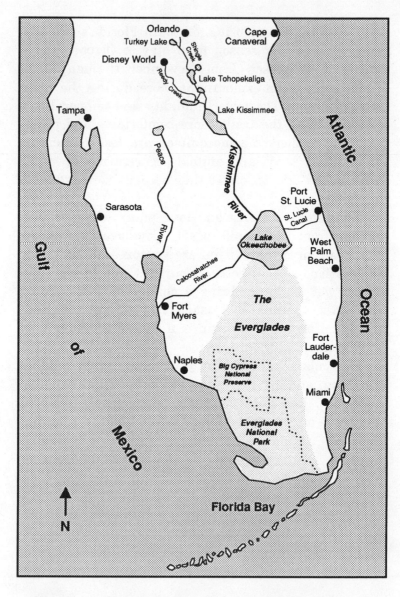

Kissimmee River-Lake Okeechobee-Everglades System

1

Anhinga Trail

An alligator sprawled on the trail ahead of me, his broad snout and heavy, black, scaly body absorbing warmth from the sun. He looked like a creature from prehistoric times, a companion of the dinosaurs. Actually, he was.

These large lizard-like animals have existed in much the same form for millions of years. Rows of scales on their backs and tails have bony *scutes* that give them an armored look. Tough, wrinkled skin connects the thick, horny scales.

Their four short, stout legs serve for locomotion on land. In water they fold them against their bodies and move by sweeping their tails from side to side. When you watch one in the water, he appears to be gliding almost without effort.

This gator was about ten feet long. Alligators have been recorded to nineteen feet, but you seldom see any longer than about twelve feet today.

The gator blinked slowly and looked lazy, but I kept a safe distance between us. Though alligators don't often attack humans, their powerful jaws and mouth full of sharp teeth can be dangerous. Their thick, muscled tail can deliver a hefty blow. In spite of a lazy look and stubby legs, an alligator can rise on its toes, lifting its body and tail, and keep up with an Olympic sprinter for short distances.

As you explore the Everglades, you'll probably see gators like this one, which I encountered as I walked along Anhinga Trail in Everglades National Park. This half-mile trail is a good place to start your exploration. You'll probably see more of the variety of Glades life here than in any place else you visit.

Anhinga Trail begins at Royal Palm Visitor Center near the national park entrance, about ten miles south of Homestead, Florida. Alligators, known as the engineers of the Everglades, are usually plentiful here in winter. But they live throughout the Glades where numerous water-filled holes — gator holes — represent the work of these engineers. To make a gator hole, an alligator finds a soft, muddy spot in the rocky floor of the Glades. He pushes out mud and plants and piles them up around the edges. The excavation then fills from below with the water that is usually close to the surface of the Glades.

An alligator will make his pool big enough to be a

comfortable home for the winter. He often travels during the wet summer but returns when the next dry season arrives. Every year the gator scoops out additional mud and plants to accommodate his growing size and to keep the hole from filling. Seeds sprout and grow in the muck he heaps around his pond to become a *tree island.*

Gator holes swarm with life during the winter months when the water-dwelling and water-feeding inhabitants of the Everglades find most of their shallow river becoming dry. Practically all animals living in the Glades make gator holes their home in the dry season.

Anhinga Trail lies alongside a man-made canal

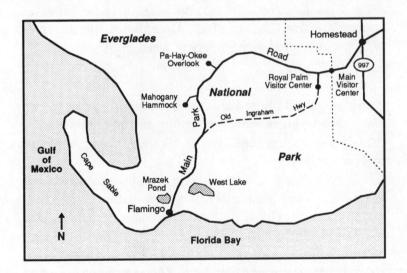

Everglades National Park - Main Park Road

dug to obtain dirt to build a road — not dug by alligators to make a home. Nevertheless, the trail gives you an idea of the creatures to be seen at a gator hole.

"Alligators eat anything that moves and some things that don't," according to one wildlife specialist. Luckily for the Glades animal life that flocks to gator holes in the dry season, that's also the time of cool winter weather. Cold-blooded alligators don't need food to keep their bodies warm. And in cold weather their activity slows, so they don't need much food for energy. In the Everglades several weeks may go by when they don't eat. In the northern parts of their range — North Florida, Georgia, Alabama, Mississippi and Louisiana — they may not eat all winter.

When the summer rains come, enough swimming, flying, running, hopping, walking, crawling and slithering creatures remain in and around gator holes to repopulate the Glades. Much Everglades life survives only because of the engineering work of alligators.

Anhinga Trail lies in Taylor Slough (pronounced slew). A *slough* is a deeper trough in the shallow river that is the Everglades. Taylor Slough flows from here to Florida Bay.

As you walk the trail, don't just concentrate on alligators. Turn your attention also to the birds sharing the slough. Great blue herons poise on stilt legs in shallow water near shore. Moorhens paddle among cattails. Often called swamp chickens, these birds cluck contentedly as they feed. You may spot a purple gallinule, his long toes spread wide, strolling over the

water on the floating leaves of lilies and spatter dock.
He searches for food among the leaves as he strolls.

As the trail heads into wetlands it becomes a
boardwalk. It takes you along the edge of saw grass
prairie. Look at some saw grass. Actually, not a grass
but a sedge (the stem is solid and not jointed), it resembles tall grass and sometimes grows twelve feet
high. Gently run your fingers down a blade, and you'll
discover where it got the *saw* in its name.

Groups of trees dot the saw grass expanse. A plac-
ard on the boardwalk rail explains these are tree islands. Nearby you see a larger mass of trees called a
hammock — an area of higher ground where trees
can grow with their roots above water even during the
wettest times. This one is a hardwood hammock.
Hammocks and tree islands are similar, but tree islands cover smaller areas than hammocks.

Willows, pond apple trees, buttonbushes and ferns
hedge the boardwalk in places. In open areas you'll
see that plant life almost covers the water with the
large leaves of spatter dock and water lilies and the
small leaves of duckweed.

In one of these open spaces pause to see if you can
spot a green-backed heron. Scan the nearby low
branches overhanging the water. They like to perch
there, motionless, scanning the water for the move-
ment of a fish. Their backs blend with the surrounding greenery, so you need to look carefully. Because of
their short legs, they prefer perching to the wading
done by the long-legged herons.

When no other visitors are on the boardwalk near
you, be still and listen. It's peaceful, but not always

quiet. Numerous large frogs, known as pig frogs may grunt lustily, sounding much like their barnyard namesakes. Perhaps a great blue heron squawks as it flies overhead.

A resounding bellow may startle you. It sounds something like the rumble of thunder or the roar of a jet plane, but it comes from the water, not the sky. That's an alligator sounding off, perhaps to warn away other gators or invite a mate. Their voices are as impressive as their appearance.

Moving along the boardwalk, you reach a wide stretch of deeper water. Numerous anhingas, the birds that give their name to this trail, usually roost during late winter and early spring in the branches of a clump of pond apple trees across the way. With binoculars you may see some of them sitting in ragged nests of twigs. If your timing is good, you may even see recently hatched young birds clamoring as their parents bring food.

Silver white plumes decorate the black backs and wings of the anhingas. You can identify the females by their buff necks. Because of their long, snaky necks, they are often called "snakebirds."

Anhingas, like most birds along this trail, eat fish. But anhingas have an unusual method of fishing — they spear fish underwater. To seek their prey, they swim below the surface for yards at a time, coming up for air and diving again.

Watch for one that has speared a fish. The anhinga surfaces with it flopping, impaled on his closed beak. To eat the fish, he flicks his flexible neck to toss it off his beak and into the air. He then catches the fish in his open beak. Occasionally, an anhinga won't be able to toss a speared fish from his beak. He then swims to the water's edge to scrape the fish off against a tree root.

Anhingas don't have as much oil on their feathers as other water birds, such as ducks. A duck's oily feathers keep water out, hold air next to its body and work like a boater's life jacket to give it buoyancy. The anhinga's lack of oil, however, makes it easier for these birds to swim underwater.

After each swim anhingas are too water-logged to fly and must dry out. When one leaves the water, it shakes like a wet dog, then spreads its wings and tail to dry. The spread tail gives anhingas another name — water turkey.

The trail circles back toward the Royal Palm Visitor Center. In the clear water of this part of the slough, you can see the fish. Their number and variety may surprise you, but they explain the presence of so many birds. A sign advises: FISHING RESERVED FOR THE BIRDS.

At the visitor center you can pause for a drink of water. Then head for the nearby Gumbo Limbo Trail.

2

Gumbo Limbo Trail

The half-mile Gumbo Limbo Trail takes you into Paradise Key Hammock where Everglades National Park had its beginnings. *Key,* as you may know, means island, and hammocks are islands in the "river of grass." Your walk should give you an idea why this hammock is known as paradise.

Leaving the open sunny area around the visitor center, the trail plunges you into the deep shade of a dense growth of tall trees. Their branches and leaves form the *canopy* high above you. Small trees and shrubs such as wax myrtle, wild coffee and tetrazygia create the *understory.* Ferns line the path and make up the *ground story.*

As soon as your eyes adjust to the dimmer light,

you will encounter a tree identified by a marker as "gumbo limbo." Park naturalists make it easy to remember and recognize by calling it "tourist tree." Its red, peeling bark resembles the skin of an unwary visitor exposed to the intense Florida sun. The gumbo limbo is one of the most prevalent trees of the hammock. The words *gumbo limbo* may be the American version of the Spanish term for its sap, *gumma elemba.*

The elevation between the Gumbo Limbo Trail and the Anhinga Trail differs by only a few inches. But each represents a different **ecosystem.** That is, the land supports a different group of plants and animals. Along the Anhinga Trail you saw only a few small, water-loving trees like willows and the pond apple. Fish and fish eaters — herons, egrets, anhingas and alligators — abounded.

Paradise Key Hammock and its Gumbo Limbo Trail are higher and somewhat drier. You may spot a few lizards scurrying among fallen leaves, and perhaps a box turtle near the path will close its shell at your approach. Footprints and scat (droppings) tell you deer and raccoons have been here. If you talk to a ranger, he or she will tell you Florida panthers and bobcats also visit this part of the park.

The hum of mosquitoes will make you glad you brought along insect repellent. Ahead, the red flash of a cardinal may cross the trail. He stays here year round. But in late winter, the hammock comes alive with the chirps, chirrs and cheeps of migrating warblers.

Shortly, you'll reach a trail-side marker identifying a *solution hole,* a rock-rimmed pond some twenty-five feet across. A pond apple tree and a willow give it shade. These wetland trees are here because of the pond. The pond is here because of the nature of the underlying rock in the southern Everglades.

Everglades rock formed a few thousand years ago when South Florida was covered by a shallow sea. This rock is limestone, not formed from coral as is generally assumed, but from a type of sand. Farther west the rock is formed from "moss animals" — tiny marine creatures which form colonies on the grasses of shallow seas.

The rock always lies close to the surface with only a thin soil covering. Its uneven surface allows slightly acid rain water to collect in low spots. Dead leaves accumulate too. Their decay adds more acid to the water. The acid dissolves the limestone, and the holes gradually become larger. Most, however, do not get as large as Deep Lake, a ninety-five-foot-deep solution hole in the Big Cypress region west of the Everglades.

Not all depressions become solution holes. Sometimes between rains the small pond dries, and its collection of moist decaying leaves becomes home for a sprouting seed. The growing seedling sends out roots which begin to break up the rock, enlarging the depression. Because the young tree uses water, moisture doesn't collect. Dead leaves and twigs pile up, break down and make soil for the growing tree.

Continue strolling along the trail. The dense shade and the moisture in the air promote the luxuriant growth of ferns, mosses and other plants that grow best in moist shade.

The strangest of the hammock's large trees is the strangler fig. A sign points out one near the trail. The strangler fig appears to be several trees with tangled roots growing over the decaying trunk of a long-dead tree. Because the dead trunk is lying flat, you may think this strangler fig probably grew here after the tree died. Quite often a fig starts its life on a living tree and eventually kills it, which explains the name "strangler."

Birds like to eat the ripe fruit of the strangler fig. The fruit is a relative of the figs grown for people. The birds sometimes carry the sticky seeds high into the branches of another tree or to the crown of a palm tree. When a seed sprouts, it starts growing as an *epiphyte* — which means it lives on air and moisture and does not take food from the tree on which it grows.

The new plant sends out long roots that eventually reach the ground. These roots grow around the support tree's trunk, branching and connecting with each other to form a network. The young fig also sends out branches and leaves which shade the support tree. Lacking sufficient sunlight and in competition with the fig's roots for food and water, the enclosed tree may eventually die. Farther along the trail, a fig tree encircles the dead remains of a palm tree, holding it upright.

If a fig seed sprouts on the ground, it grows without a support tree just as a typical tree does.

Deep in the hammock are some mighty live oak trees, their wide-spreading branches shaggy with epiphytes such as orchids and *bromeliads*.

Not all plants thrive in the shade of the hammock

floor. Some, seeking space or sunlight, have adapted to growing as epiphytes, and live oaks provide them a good home.

Live oak branches grow out, horizontally, rather than up, and the bark has deep ridges. The seeds of epiphyte plants catch in the bark and their roots hold. Epiphytes grow on other varieties of trees, but on live oaks they often cloak the tree like a fur coat.

Ferns, orchids and bromeliads cover the branches above you. Bromeliads may seem to be the most abundant, or perhaps they just appear more spectacular than the ferns and the orchids if not in bloom. While a few orchids flower in winter, most bloom in spring or summer. They are smaller than the large commercial orchids you might buy at a florist.

Bromeliads, a group of mostly tropical plants, may live as epiphytes or as *terrestrial* plants — growing on the ground. The best known terrestrial bromeliad is the pineapple. Many epiphytic bromeliads are called wild pines because they look like pineapples.

Try to spot one type of wild pine in particular, the quill leaf — also called cardinal wild pine or stiff-leaved wild pine. Look for one growing low enough on a tree so you can examine it. The stiff, slender, foot-long, pointed leaves rise from a base, overlapping and forming a water-tight cup. In the center, rising a foot or two above the leaves, is a stalk that flowers with bright red bracts. In spring or summer purple flowers emerge from these bracts, and yellow stamens show beyond the petals.

The water-tight cup of the leaf base usually holds enough water, replenished by dew, to last the plant

during the dry season. The water in the cup also supplies many other creatures. Bacteria and tiny plants
known as algae live in the water. Insects visit for both
water and food, and mosquitoes come to lay eggs. The
larvae, the mosquitoes, the insects and the water all
attract snakes, birds, frogs and other creatures looking for food and water. Tadpoles may develop, feed
and become food. Some tiny creatures may die and
add their bodies to this "soup." This air plant supports
a miniature tree-limb ecosystem.

In the dry winter season, you can see the curled,
brown, dry fronds of resurrection ferns on live oak
branches. The ferns look dead. But after a rain the
fronds will uncurl and become green again. All the
plants of this wet/dry-cycle land have some way of
coping with the dry period, just as plants farther
north adjust to the cold season.

Beyond the epiphyte-laden oak trees the trail intersects the overgrown remains of the Old Ingraham
Highway, which once went from Miami to Flamingo.
A majestic royal palm rises above the other hammock
trees that shade the road. At one time there were
enough of them to give this hammock an alternate
name — Royal Palm Hammock. If you were standing
back away from the hammock, you would see others,
here and there, towering above the canopy.

To people unfamiliar with tropical vegetation, a
palm tree may appear to be just a palm tree. They
don't realize that an estimated three thousand species

exist worldwide, although only a few of these grow naturally in Florida.

Palms are ancient plants, dating back some fifty-five million years. Most don't have branches. Their leaves, called *fronds,* grow at the top of a pithy trunk. If you were to cut across a trunk, you would not see growth rings as you would on the trunks of other trees.

The trunks of royal palms resemble grey concrete pillars supporting a few feet of green at the top. Royal palms can grow to 125 feet tall. Their fronds range from twelve to twenty-five feet long. The palm you're looking at isn't 125 feet tall, but it does top the surrounding trees by many feet.

Leaving the royal palm, walk along the old highway away from the Gumbo Limbo Trail, which loops back to the visitor center.

Efforts to protect this largest hammock of the Everglades resulted in the dedication of Royal Palm State Park in 1916. A lodge and other buildings belonging to that park stood along this portion of the old road. But you'll find only a few traces — a small building in the former deer park and some orange trees.

Actually, the first moves to conserve Everglades plants and animals began before 1900. The railroad, built along Florida's eastern coast, had reached Miami, and the expansion and development of that resort city had begun. But some conservation-minded people began to see that development and the Everglades were not a good mix.

When Royal Palm State Park was established, it became the seed from which Everglades National Park would grow. The decades between the first idea and the dedication of Everglades National Park in 1947 were years of continuous effort on the part of many individuals who believed the biological treasures of the area should be preserved.

Everglades National Park was the first to be created for the purpose of preserving living things within its boundaries. Other parks, such as Yellowstone, Yosemite, Grand Canyon and Smoky Mountains, were designed to protect scenic and geologic areas. The protection of plants and animals was secondary.

Marjory Stoneman Douglas, a respected supporter of the Everglades and author of *The Everglades: River of Grass,* pointed out in the beginning of her book that the world has no other Everglades. It is not duplicated anywhere else. The Everglades, according to Douglas, is — and always has been — one of the world's unique regions.

Recognition of this uniqueness has brought the park designations as an International Biosphere Reserve, a World Heritage Site and a Wetland of International Importance. Visitors to the park come from all over the world. Along the trails you'll probably hear conversations and exclamations in many languages.

Retrace your steps on the Old Ingraham Highway to where you left the Gumbo Limbo Trail. Continue along the trail a short distance to return to the visitor center.

Your walk along Anhinga and Gumbo Limbo trails introduced you to some of the plants and animals that are being preserved. Now, leaving the Royal Palm Visitor Center, drive west along the Main Park Road for about ten miles to Pa-Hay-Okee Overlook to see more.

3

Pa-Hay-Okee Overlook

On the drive to the Pa-Hay-Okee Overlook you'll see a freshwater marl prairie. *Marl,* composed of dissolved limestone and clay, is the soil on which the saw grass grows. The prairie, with saw grass growing as far as you can see, is what visitors generally expect of the Everglades.

The word *glade* comes from an Old English word *glyde* or *glaed* meaning a bright open space in a forest. The name *Everglades* was first used for this area by an Englishman in 1823. Possibly he used the *ever* because they appear to go on forever.

The name *Everglades* used in its narrowest sense means this saw grass prairie. In a broader use it in-

cludes other plant communities in South Florida: pinelands, hammocks, cypress swamps and mangrove
estuaries that border the prairie. All these plant communities exist in Everglades National Park.

As you drive you'll also see pinelands. Most visitors do not expect pinelands in the Everglades. In
fact, people usually do not even think of pines when
they think of Florida trees. But they are one of the
most common and most valuable trees in the state.

Slash pines are the only pines in the Everglades.
The most common understory plant of the pinelands
is saw palmetto. These are low-growing palms whose
trunks sprawl along the ground. Both slash pine and
saw palmetto are fire resistant, a characteristic that
allows pine forests to survive. If a pineland is not
burned occasionally, a hardwood hammock will replace it. Pine seedlings require much sun to thrive.
But hardwood seedlings growing under the pine trees
can shade out pine seedlings. As the old pine trees die,
hardwoods take over and a hammock stands where
there was once a pineland. A fire, however, kills
young hardwoods and gives pine seedlings a chance.

If a fire has burned any of the pines you see along
the road, they may show blackened trunks where the
flames touched them, but their high branches are
probably now fresh and green. A tough, thick outer
bark protects the inner life-sustaining tissues. Saw
palmettos under the pines also quickly become green
again. Their deep roots and thick stem help them survive.

In the past, nature took care of the burning by
setting fires with lightening strikes. Now, in the park,

pinelands are preserved by prescribed burns. Rangers schedule and set these burns at times when the fire can be controlled and burn only where it is needed. They usually schedule burns during the wet season.

Naturalists in Everglades National Park pioneered the use of prescribed burns in 1958. Such burns are now used in other national parks as a means of preserving ecological systems and for preventing accidentally started fires from burning out of control. When an abundance of dead plants and dry leaves build up they could feed a devastating blaze.

Although the hammocks, like Royal Palm which you visited along the Gumbo Limbo Trail, are slightly raised and dry, wet areas usually surround them. Their deep shade allows hammocks to hold much moisture which protects them from burning. Taylor Slough, for example, protects part of Royal Palm Hammock.

On your drive, you'll approach a roadside sign that says: ROCK REEF PASS ELEVATION 3 FEET (0.9 METERS). The sign typically prompts jokes about the need for oxygen masks and mock complaints of popping ears. This little ridge emphasizes the low-lying nature of the park's terrain. Its highest altitude is a lofty ten feet above sea level.

Beyond the pass, the vegetation changes to include dwarf or pond cypress scattered about the prairie. These small trees lose their feathery, needlelike leaves in the fall. In late winter they begin to show green, their new leaves as soft and light as the down of baby birds. In summer they will be green and thriving. Although they are conifers — as are pines, hemlocks and fir trees — cypress trees lose their leaves in winter.

Most biologists think these small trees are the same species as the towering bald cypress. The dwarf cypresses grow slowly and are stunted by poor growing conditions. Although small, some of these trees may be hundreds of years old.

Off the main road, widely spaced cypress trees line the side road to Pa-Hay-Okee Overlook Trail. It is a short trail, about a quarter mile, which leads to an observation tower. *Pa-Hay-Okee* is Indian and means grassy waters. And because these are the grassy waters, most of the trail is actually a boardwalk. Just how much water you'll see under the walk depends on the season. At the height of the wet season several inches of water may cover all the land. But as the dry season approaches, only an inch or two may sit under the walk, or the ground might even be completely dry.

Masses of greenish-yellow **periphyton** float in the water and cover the ground. Made up of algae and some tiny one-celled animals, periphyton is like a sponge. Even when the Everglades seem completely dry you can usually pick up a bit and squeeze water from it. Only extreme drought conditions will dry it out entirely.

Periphyton, with the algae that make up most of its mass, performs tremendously important services for the Glades. One of the algae's jobs is to carry on a process called *photosynthesis.* Algae are mostly green plants that contain chlorophyll, which must be present for photosynthesis to occur. Through this process algae manufacture food by taking sun energy, changing it and storing it as chemical energy.

As food makers, algae are the base of a complicated food web. Mosquito larvae, tadpoles and other tiny animals feed on the algae. Many of the algae-feeders are in turn eaten by small animals and fish. These are then eaten by larger animals such as birds, raccoons and alligators.

Algae also take calcium, which is plentiful in Glades water, and change it to the marl, or soil, in which saw grass grows.

When saw grass dies it helps make peat which allows other plants to sprout and grow. The peat may build up above the water level to support tree islands in the grassy river. These islands are sometimes called heads. Depending on the predominant kind of tree, they may be willow heads, bay heads or cypress heads.

The peat and other decaying plants form acid which then dissolves calcium from the original marl, and the calcium is available for the algae to start the cycle again.

Move along the walkway and climb the few steps to

the overlook tower. You can now look across the
Glades and see the vast saw grass prairie extending
to the horizon. Here and there tree islands break the
expanse.

A display board in the center of the tower platform
helps you understand more about the Everglades. A
map of southern Florida shows Lake Okeechobee at
the top. It is a large lake, the largest in Florida, and
second only to Lake Michigan in the United States.

Before settlers moved into southern Florida, Lake
Okeechobee overflowed when it was full. The water
moved slowly south to the tip of Florida, where it
joined Florida Bay between the Atlantic Ocean and
the Gulf of Mexico.

The water stayed mostly in the center of the Florida peninsula because a ridge of higher land runs
along each side near the coasts. The land between
Lake Okeechobee and Florida Bay slopes so gradually,
only an inch or two each mile, that the water moved
very slowly. It formed a wide shallow river, about six
inches deep, fifty miles wide and a hundred miles
long. Because it was shallow and slow moving, saw
grass and other plants were able to grow in its bed.
This was the Everglades — the river of grass.

Then the settlers came. Canals were dug, drawing
off much of the water flow. Farms were started on the
drained land, and large cities grew along the coasts.
Roads were built across the Everglades, becoming, in
effect, dams. Little of the river still flows today. Here
at Pa-Hay-Okee you can see a bit of that river. It
moves so slowly you can't tell it is moving, but move it
does.

The loss of natural flow causes problems for Everglades National Park and the plants and animals the park is supposed to preserve. Later in your explorations you'll visit Lake Okeechobee to find out why the canals were built. You'll also then learn about a "Save Our Everglades" program that has plans for adjusting and restoring much of the natural flow.

Before you leave the Pa-Hay-Okee area, consider exploring a cypress head. Pick a large one close to the highway where the Pa-Hay-Okee side road and the Main Park Road intersect.

Though many small cypress trees are spread here and there about the prairie, some grow in rounded clumps. These trees are bigger than the scattered ones. Cypress heads develop in depressions in the limestone where water and decayed plant material — peat — collect. The depression is deeper in the center and more of the nourishing peat collects there. Consequently, trees in the center of the clump grow taller giving it the look of a dome. So the heads are also called cypress domes.

Other tree islands are on ground higher than the prairie. But cypress domes are located in low spots, so to explore one you will have to go wading. You will need to wear sneakers and long pants and have dry clothing into which you can change afterwards.

Entering the dome, you'll once again step from bright sunlight into deep shade. You may almost feel like you are going into a church or cathedral, dark and quiet with sunlight filtering through the canopy as though through stained glass. Straight tall trunks of cypresses draw your eyes upward. The foliage of many epiphytes appears green, but their flowering stalks may create spots of color.

The water is dark, a sort of tea from decaying leaves. The bottom is soft with these leaves, but firm enough that you won't sink in. As you move deeper into the dome, perhaps you'll spot a green tree frog clinging to a branch or a lizard scurrying away. You probably won't see any snakes, but keep a wary eye. If any poisonous water moccasins are around, you don't want to take them by surprise.

Few Everglades visitors make their way into a cypress dome, although park rangers lead occasional "wet walks." Snakes are one reason few people dare to go wading, but snakes are shy creatures and will usually retreat if they sense human presence.

You probably won't see any alligators, either. But it's always a possibility wherever there is water in the Glades. If you do, keep your distance and do not approach too closely. No visitor has ever been injured by either a snake or an alligator in the park. The most hazardous beast of the Everglades is the mosquito. Visitors are bitten practically daily.

When you leave the cypress head, you'll feel the experience was well worth getting your feet wet.

Your next explorations will take you deeper into the park to see more of its plant and animal life. You'll also learn of a man who was murdered while protecting Everglades birds.

4

Road to Flamingo

From Pa-Hay-Okee continue along the Main Park
Road, which now curves south. You're heading toward
Flamingo, about twenty-five miles away. But there
are a couple of short side trails you will want to explore as you go.

Once as I was traveling this road, about a mile or
two after leaving Pa-Hay-Okee, I saw something moving in the road ahead. I slowed and then pulled over.
A large diamondback rattlesnake was starting to
cross the road but had stopped and coiled as cars approached. He looked big enough to match the record
eight feet for his species.

Dark brown, diamond-shaped blotches, banded
with black and white, decorated his gray, rough-
scaled back. Black and white stripes marked the sides

of his head. His tail sported a series of rattles. He was as beautiful in his own way as the much more admired birds.

Other cars stopped and soon a small crowd had gathered. The coiled snake waited, watching the group, then glided away into the roadside underbrush.

Fear of snakes shouldn't stop anyone from visiting the Everglades. Most visitors never encounter one. And if they do, the snake retreats as this one did. At no time was he dangerous. His coiling was defensive, in case the onlookers proved hostile. His wait, because of the gathered people, seemed designed to allow him to determine the best way to escape. Of course, we all kept a respectful distance. If we had approached too closely and the snake felt threatened, he might have decided to strike.

Mahogany Hammock

Your next stop is Mahogany Hammock. Here, too, you'll step from bright sunlight into the cool shade of tropical growth. This half-mile path slopes upward from the saw grass prairie more noticeably than the Gumbo Limbo Trail. But as there, a ground story of ferns and shrubs blankets the earth.

Because the wood of the West Indian mahogany is hard, strong, durable and close-grained, it's called the prince of woods. As a result the trees are cut and used for fine furniture. Few are left in Florida. In this hammock a champion mahogany tree, twelve feet around and ninety feet tall, stands among other giants. Isolation first protected these trees from loggers. By the time the road was built, the park owned the hammock and protected them.

Mahogany seed pods, the size of large plums, grow up from the branch instead of hanging down. If you pick up the remains of a fallen pod, you find it holds a closely packed mass of seeds each with a wing, or vane, to help it sail on the wind.

This hammock shows the effects of a hurricane. Huge tree trunks lie on the ground, their roots torn from the thin soil. As in all the southern Everglades, rock lies close to the surface, and tree roots spread out rather than going deep. The rangers do not cut up and haul away the remains of these fallen giants. They know that nature makes good use of all dead material.

Take a close look at one of the dead trunks. You'll find it covered with ferns, mushrooms, mosses and lichens. But it's not just a place for plants to perch, it's another Everglades miniature ecosystem. Microscopic life causes the trunk to decay, thus providing food, or nutrients, for the plant life. Insects live among the plants, and a small lizard may make a meal of one. Later a bird may eat the lizard.

Very gently lift a piece of decaying bark. You'll probably find insect eggs and larvae. Carefully replace the bark so as not to disturb the insect nest. Birds, including migrating warblers in spring and fall, search for insect eggs and larvae to eat.

West Lake Trail

Back on the road, continue south to West Lake. When

you think of lakes, you naturally think of fresh water.
But West Lake, connected to saltwater Florida Bay by
a narrow waterway, has **brackish** water. Brackish
water is found where sea and fresh water mix, and so
the water has salt content but less so than sea water.
You are now near where the fresh water from the
river of grass joins the ocean.

A half-mile boardwalk along the lake shore will
take you through a mangrove community. Informative
signs along the way help you to recognize the different
mangrove species and gain an understanding of their
importance

There are four different species of trees in this
community — buttonwood, red mangrove, black mangrove and white mangrove. Although each is a different family, they are alike because they can grow in or
near salt water.

The buttonwood, even though it does not have
mangrove in its name, is sometimes called the fourth
mangrove. It grows in salty but dry soil. So it usually
grows landward of the three mangrove species, a little
farther from the salt water. Its seeds grow in small
button-like cones.

All mangroves grow intermingled, but white mangrove resembles buttonwood by growing a little away
from the water. Red and black mangroves can thrive
with salt water around their roots. Black mangroves
grow in tidal areas so they are not continuously surrounded by water, while red mangroves grow in shallow salt water.

You can learn to distinguish red and black mangroves by their easily recognizable features. White

mangroves and buttonwoods do not have such distinctive characteristics.

Black mangroves have dark bark. In the muck around them you'll find hundreds of projections, about the size of pencils, growing from their roots. Called *pneumatophores* (pronounced new-MAT-uh-fors), these projections provide oxygen to the roots.

Red mangroves are most often the trees you see growing out into the water. They have reddish, arching "prop" roots growing from their trunks. Prop roots carry oxygen to the underwater roots and enable the trees to live in shifting sand, tides and waves.

Besides prop roots, red mangroves have developed another way to deal with their environment. Most plants drop their seeds on land, where the seed sprouts and starts a new tree. But a red mangrove is surrounded by salt water or salty mud flats in which its seeds can't germinate. So the red mangrove's seeds sprout and start growing a new plant while still hanging from a branch.

The seed grows into a cigar-shaped seedling whose outer covering lets in water but filters out salt. Botanists call these seeds and seedlings *propagules.* If the propagule drops into the mud, it will stick upright and continue to grow. If it falls into the water, it floats and may be carried hundreds of miles away. At first the propagule floats flat on the water, continuing to grow. The root end, however, gradually becomes heavier until the propagule floats straight up. When it reaches a shallow spot, the root tip catches. The roots grow, penetrating deeper into the bottom, and soon it becomes a small tree.

In some parts of the Everglades, red mangroves once grew to a height of nearly a hundred feet. These at West Lake are about thirty or forty feet tall. Notice the twenty-foot stumps of trees broken off by a hurricane. These stumps continue to send up branches and flaunt greenery. Judging from the diameter of the remaining trunks, they formerly towered to lofty heights.

The roots of each mangrove crisscross those of its neighbors in tangled profusion. A grove of mangroves is not a place to take a stroll. The boardwalk at West Lake lets you visit an area you otherwise would find almost impossible to penetrate.

Many Floridians once considered mangrove forests a waste of valuable shoreline property. Some short-sighted landowners and developers still do. They would like to bulldoze the trees and fill the land to build homes and office buildings. But studies by naturalists show the incalculable value of these forests, and they are now protected by law.

Mangroves, with their tangled roots and pneumatophores, trap and hold — despite the force of winds and tides — sand, dropped leaves, twigs, seaweed and grasses. This once-living material, called *detritus*, is food for bacteria and numerous minute sea creatures. Fish fry (young fish), shrimp larvae, baby crabs and lobsters, feed on the bacteria and sea creatures. The jungle of prop roots and pneumatophores protect them from larger fish. This nursery includes the young of many ocean fish important to the fishing industry, sport fishermen and to all who include seafood in their diets.

A mangrove forest is especially valuable as a home for birds — a *rookery* where large groups of birds return each night to rest or build nests and raise young. Birds often choose island mangroves for nesting rather than shoreline forests. An island offers some protection from raccoons who will feast on bird eggs if they find them.

Hermit crabs, land crabs, mangrove snakes and mangrove terrapins live here at West Lake. Coon oysters grow on the prop roots, and raccoons love to eat them. In Florida Bay, sea turtles feed on mangrove leaves growing close to the water.

It is possible to see both alligators and crocodiles at West Lake. But crocodiles are rare and are in danger of becoming extinct in this country. Both federal and state governments have classified them as endangered.

American crocodiles also live near islands in the Caribbean and along the northern coast of South America, but they are becoming rare in these habitats as well. All that remain in the United States are in South Florida, and most of those are in Florida Bay. Estimates of their number range from three hundred to five hundred. The section of bay where most crocodiles live is a sanctuary which is closed to the public.

Crocodiles and alligators look a lot alike, but there are differences. Crocodiles have gray, grayish green or grayish brown hides, alligators black. A crocodile's snout is narrow and its teeth protrude. An alligator's snout is broad and its teeth are covered when the mouth is closed. Because crocodiles prefer salt or brackish water and alligators prefer fresh, the two

seldom meet. But even though the water is slightly
brackish in West Lake, rangers say they frequently
see a large alligator here.

Your walk along the boardwalk takes you in a
circle, through the mangroves to a viewing platform
on the lake and then back through more mangroves to
the parking lot.

Mrazek Pond

The last stop you'll make before Flamingo is Mrazek
Pond, a popular bird-watching spot in winter because
it is a favorite feeding area for birds. You may see a
few birds here anytime of the year, but they become
most numerous for two or three weeks in the dry season when the water reaches a particular, ideal low
level, usually in February. Drying of the Everglades
during the winter concentrates fish where water remains. And the birds will stay at the pond until
they've fished it out or until the water gets too low for
most fish to survive.

Crowds of winter visitors often gather along the
shore to watch crowds of wading and swimming birds
in the small roadside pond. Great egrets, snowy
egrets, great blue herons, little blue herons, tri-colored herons, American coots, moorhens, wood storks,
green-backed herons, white ibis, and blue-winged teal
all enjoy what must be a multitude of fishes to feed
such a throng of birds.

Alligators are here, too. The pond is a good model
of a gator hole, although it is larger than a single
alligator would build.

The birds feed happily, unmindful of the onlookers or the clicking of camera shutters. On rare occasions a gasp of dismay rises from some of the observers, and fingers point to the toes of a bird disappearing into the mouth of an alligator. The rest of the feeding birds are undisturbed.

But that's an uncommon event for visitors to see. Alligators seldom eat in the daylight. It's even more uncommon in winter when they eat little.

Flamingo

Flamingo is as far south as you can drive in the mainland United States. A former fishing village, Flamingo no longer exists as a town. But it does have visitor services, including a lodge, a marina and a campground. Two adjacent two-story buildings house a park visitor center and museum in one and a gift shop and restaurant in the other. Galleries on each level, which connect the two buildings, overlook Florida Bay.

Visit the upper gallery. From here the shallow waters of the bay shimmer blue-green in the sunlight and are dappled with deep-green mangrove-covered islands. Directly in front of you, a vegetationless sandbar shows above the water at low tide. The sandbar may then be almost covered with small wading birds such as sandpipers, plovers, stilts and willits. A few large white birds may stand out.

Public spotting scopes, more powerful than binoculars, make observing easy. The largest birds would be white pelicans, about four-feet long with a wingspan of nine feet. Near them you may spot some slightly smaller brown pelicans.

White pelicans are winter visitors to the Everglades. They summer in western North America — Yellowstone National Park is one place to find them nesting.

Walk to the marina for a closer look at brown pelicans. They hang around there looking for handouts from fishermen. Almost every pile — the posts that support the docks — will have a pelican. Those piles with no pelicans will be serving as pedestals for gulls, there for the same reason as the pelicans.

Brown pelicans may grow to three-and-a-half-feet long and have a wingspan of six-and-a-half feet. Their best-known feature is their long bills with deep pouches.

Scan the sky. You may spot several flying in line with their characteristic "flap, flap, flap, glide" flight pattern. One of the pelicans may peel off and dive head first with a splash into the canal between the marina and the bay. He'll probably come up with a fish in his pouch, the tail perhaps flopping out, and may disappear into the mangroves on the opposite bank of the canal. More often he will drop his beak to drain out water and then swallow the fish while he rests on the water's surface.

The marina gives you an opportunity to take to the water. Concession boats depart to tour the interior wilderness and Florida Bay as far as Cape Sable, the mainland's southernmost point. Rental boats, canoes and charter craft are also available. If you would rather stick to the land, a tram runs from Flamingo to

Snake Bight, a nearby bay, for a closer look at shore-birds.

Outside the visitor center, take a minute to look at the bronze plaque commemorating Guy Bradley, the first Audubon warden to be killed protecting Everglades rookeries.

In the 1880s and '90s fashionable ladies adorned their hats with bird feathers, sometimes whole stuffed birds. The breeding plumes of great and snowy egrets were especially favored, and men made money killing egrets for their plumes.

These "plumers" would find a rookery, wait until the birds were nesting and kill all the adult birds. They left the young and the eggs to die or be eaten by predators. Plumers chose nesting time because the birds would not fly away and abandon their nests. In addition, at nesting time the plumes were at their finest. Plumers slaughtered thousands of birds, annihilating entire rookeries.

Leaders of the National Association of Audubon Societies, now the National Audubon Society, were outraged. They persuaded the Florida legislature to outlaw the killing of these birds, but were not able to get provisions for money to enforce the law. So Audubon societies raised money to pay wardens to protect the remaining rookeries.

Guy Bradley became one of the wardens. One day he caught plumers in the act of taking dead birds from a rookery island. When he attempted to arrest them, one of the plumers shot him and left him to die a lingering death in his drifting boat. At his trial the killer claimed Bradley shot first. And even though no bullets had been fired from the warden's gun, the man went free.

A few years later Audubon representatives influenced the state of New York, where the plumes were being purchased, to outlaw the trade. That ended the plundering of rookeries in time to prevent extermintion of the last egrets.

Consider spending the night in Flamingo, either at the Flamingo Lodge or the campground. But make reservations for the lodge well in advance by telephoning the Flamingo Ranger Station at 305-253-2241 or 813-695-3101. You can also write to P.O. Box 428, Flamingo, FL 33030. Campground spaces are not reserved.

Be sure you awake early to watch the sunrise. Typically, streaks of pink, mauve, rose and lavender interspersed with a few gray clouds light the sky and reflect in the waters of Florida Bay. The rising edge of the sun may tint with rose the white feathers of a wading great egret.

As the sun grows to a flaming globe, a whoosh of wingbeats overhead may catch your attention. Hundreds of white ibis commute at this time of day from their mangrove-island rookeries in the bay to inland feeding areas. They come in groups, flying so low you feel you could almost reach up and touch them. The rustle of air through the black-bordered wings of these large white birds serves as a fitting accompaniment to the beginning of another day in the Everglades.

You are now going to move your explorations to the northern sections of Everglades National Park. But you'll have to make a wide detour to get there. Retrace your route along Main Park Road back to the entrance. Leave the park and head for State Road 997 going north to U.S. 41 — the Tamiami Trail. You'll take the Tamiami Trail west to visit Shark Valley, an Indian village and the Ten Thousand Islands.

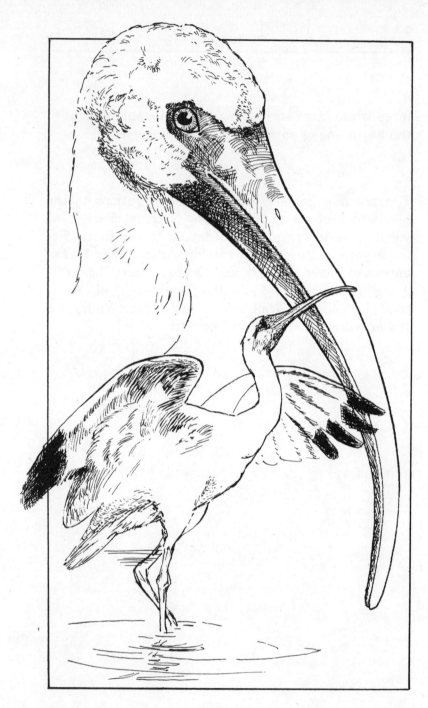

White ibis

Green-backed heron

Red mangrove prop roots, inset: propagules

Snowy egret

Great egret

Anhinga

Upper: brown pelican, lower: white pelicans

Great blue heron

5

Tamiami Trail

The Tamiami Trail stretches ahead of you straight and flat to the horizon. Behind, as you head west, sprawl the growing tentacles of the city of Miami. The Trail goes to Naples on Florida's Gulf Coast and then follows the coast to Tampa. The name *Tamiami* comes from the cities at each end.

The Trail was the first of only two roads that cross the Everglades. Started in 1916, it was not completed until 1928. Many obstacles slowed the building of this two-lane causeway across the river of grass. Learning how to build in the mucky wetland was a matter of trial and error. Workers braved swarming mosquitoes and slithering water moccasins. Torrential tropical downpours alternated with blistering blazing sun. World War I stopped work for a time, but eventually the road was completed.

Tall, graceful Australian pine trees line the right side of the Trail. These beautiful trees, along with two other introduced tree species — the melaleuca or punk tree (also from Australia) and the Brazilian pepper — are a threat to the Everglades. Adapting well to Everglades growing conditions and without enemies to control their spread, these "exotic" trees crowd out native plants.

Australian pines aren't actually pines. They got that name because their slender twigs look like pine needles. The tree has leaves that appear as tiny bracts along the "needles." Besides crowding out the native plants, Australian pines have shallow roots and blow over easily in strong winds. Their brittle branches also break off in storms. And their fallen needles leach chemicals that prevent anything growing under them.

Perhaps the most serious exotic threat to the Everglades is the melaleuca. Thick stands of these trees grow profusely in the wetlands. They got a head start when seeds were spread by airplane to help dry up the Everglades. Drying up the Everglades was once the major aim of South Floridians. Melaleuca trees soak up and *transpire* (evaporate through their leaves) quantities of water.

When a melaleuca is cut or burned it releases millions of tiny seeds. The trees grow so closely together practically nothing can get through. Little wildlife will live in melaleuca thickets. Few birds nest in them.

They bloom throughout the year, and the pollen causes severe breathing problems in some people.

Brazilian pepper has masses of attractive red berries around the Christmas season, so it is sometimes called Florida holly, an undeserved name. It is neither a native Florida tree nor a holly. It's a member of the poison ivy family, and sensitive people develop a rash from contact.

Birds and mammals seem to like eating the tree's berries, sometimes with sad results. The berries contain a chemical that drugs the animals, so they may have fatal accidents. Occasionally the drug itself may cause death to birds, young deer or raccoons. When the seeds pass through the digestive systems of animals, they are dropped ready to grow, spreading the Brazilian pepper's range.

As much as funds permit, park rangers work to prevent the spread of these three trees in Everglades National Park and in the Big Cypress National Preserve which lies north and west of the park.

Shark Valley

A stop at Shark Valley — about seventeen miles along after turning onto the Tamiami Trail — gives you a close-up look at the center of the Everglades. Water coming from Lake Okeechobee once moved through this wide, shallow slough — Shark Valley Slough — into the Shark River to flow southwest to the Gulf of Mexico. Today, the water no longer moves freely. Canals and flood gates control its flow.

Sharks coming from the gulf into the lower river

give both the river and the slough their names.

Private automobiles are not allowed along the fifteen-mile Shark Valley Loop road which leads out to an observation tower. You'll have to park your car at the entrance and visit by tram, bicycle or on foot. The park's two-hour tram ride offers a good way to explore the area. A naturalist aboard the tram identifies the plants and animals along the loop road.

If you take the tram tour near the end of the dry season, you may see numerous turkey vultures, often called buzzards. Well into the dry season low water levels kill large numbers of fish. The vultures clean up the remains, otherwise you would probably find the trip uncomfortably smelly.

It's not unusual for the tram to stop so passengers can watch white-tailed deer, perhaps a mother and fawn peering from the shrubbery. Like other wildlife in protected places, the deer seem to realize they will not be harmed. Instead of fleeing, after noting your presence they may return to nibbling leaves.

White-tailed deer abound throughout the eastern United States. Everglades deer differ from their northern cousins, however, in being smaller with broader hoofs that don't sink into the muck. These deer also have a resistance to hoof rot which affects most hoofed animals in wet conditions.

At a "borrow pit" where rock was removed to build the road, you can leave the tram briefly. Most South Florida roads feature roadside canals. When fill for the road is dug, the resulting canal serves for drainage. But if more than usual fill is needed, a borrow pit is the answer.

Just as the gator hole along Anhinga Trail was dug by man, this borrow pit serves as another man-made gator hole. Turtles and alligators bask on its banks. Great blue and little blue herons, tri-colored herons, great egrets and anhingas feed in its water.

Your next stop is the sixty-five-foot observation tower at the loop road's turnaround point. From the spiraling, concrete tower you can see for miles. As at Pa-Hay-Okee, saw grass prairie reaches to the horizon. During the dry season, here and there the teardrop contours of tree islands embroider a deep green into the dry, yellow-green saw grass. In the expanse of azure sky a few fluffy white clouds may border the horizon. Except, perhaps, in the west where a gray cloud bank promises a chance of a shower for the dry land. Even in the dry season some rain falls in the Glades.

A canal at the tower's base is generally full of alligators, particularly in winter. The gators lie flank to flank in the shallows or along the banks. This is another place that serves as a refuge for animals when the glades are dry. Willows grow along the canal's edge, and cattails, alligator flag and pickerel weed grow in the water.

Back on the tram, continue to be alert for wildlife on the return trip. Sometimes you can spot an otter, his bright black eyes glistening and his whiskered nose sniffing, before the water-loving animal's sleek brown body slips away.

After the tram ride, you can explore on foot a trail leading through a small hammock and a boardwalk running through wetlands. When you're ready to

leave Shark Valley, you'll return to the Tamiami Trail
to go west about a thousand feet to a Miccosukee (pronounced mick-uh-SUE-key) Indian village located on
a reservation adjoining the national park.

The Miccosukee Indians

Although sometimes called Seminoles, those Indians
living in South Florida — including along the Tamiami Trail — call themselves Miccosukee. The other
Indians living in Florida are Seminoles but not
Miccosukee.

Neither of these Indian groups are descended from
the tribes who lived in this part of Florida when the
Spanish arrived in the 1500s. Those were the Tequestas in the southeast and the Calusas in the southwest.

In 1565 the Spanish made the first permanent set-
tlement in what was to become Florida in the northern part of the state at Saint Augustine. In South
Florida, the Spanish gave up on any idea of exploring
the interior. They found it forbidding and thought it
worthless.

The two original Florida tribes, the Tequestas and
the Calusas, began to die out. Some of the Indians
were captured and made slaves, many were killed by
diseases brought by Spanish explorers. Foreign diseases were deadly because the Indians had no natural
immunity against them. It is possible that a few of
these native Indians were absorbed into the Seminoles who started moving into the area about the time
the Tequestas and Calusas disappeared.

Beginning in the early 1700s, white settlers moving into what was to become the southern United States drove the Indians from their lands. Most moved west, but some of the Creek tribes in Georgia migrated south into Florida. In the language of some Indians, such people were called *Sim-in-oli,* meaning "wild." These were the Indians we now know as the Seminoles.

The Florida territory became part of the United States in 1821 and a state in 1845. And as settlers moved into North and Central Florida, the Seminoles moved deeper down the Florida peninsula. But the U.S. government decided to move all the Seminoles out West. The Army was assigned to round them up and carry out the move. Many of the Seminoles refused to go, and through 1858 periodic Indians wars ensued.

Eventually, the Army managed to move most of the Seminoles, but a few continued to resist, fleeing into the Everglades. Soldiers attempted to pursue them. But the sharp saw grass, the wet ground and the hordes of mosquitoes made the area uninviting. Nobody objected to letting the last of the Indians remain there.

Those hundred-and-fifty to two-hundred Indians who remained free in the Everglades, developed a way of life adapted to the swampy land. Their descendants now number about three thousand. Even today a few of them live much as they did before the Tamiami Trail brought the modern world to them. By visiting this village you'll get some idea of that way of life.

The Miccosukee dwellings, called **chickees,** have

no walls. Four corner posts support a roof made of
palm-leaf thatch. The floor is raised a foot or two
above the ground to keep the occupants above water
in the worst of storms. The Indians also placed their
villages on the highest ground they could find to help
prevent flooding in the chickees.

Early Indians traveled the Everglades in dugout
canoes made from large cypress logs. Some were big
enough to accommodate a whole family. They seldom
use canoes today, preferring airboats instead. You'll
learn more about these craft later.

The Miccosukee developed distinctive clothing.
The women wear full, gathered patchwork skirts. The
patchwork is similar to that in quilts, but the Indians
use pieces sometimes only a fraction of an inch wide.
Jackets for men are made from the same kind of
piecework. The Indians usually make the clothing on
hand-powered sewing machines.

The village gift shop sells these handmade skirts
and jackets to earn income for the people. You'll also
find: dolls the women make from the fibrous sheath of
palm fronds and then dress in delicate patchwork cos-
tumes, Indian handiwork from around the United
States, posters, postcards and other souvenir items.

Each year in late December this village hosts a
festival. Representatives from many American Indian
tribes come to perform dances and to display and sell
handicrafts.

As you continue to travel west on the Tamiami Trail,
through the Big Cypress National Preserve and on to

the Ten Thousand Islands, you'll pass other small Indian villages, some with gift shops, restaurants and airboat rides.

6

Ten Thousand Islands

To reach the western part of Everglades National
Park and the Ten Thousand Islands, you must drive
through the Big Cypress National Preserve. The National Park Service oversees preserves but they differ
from national parks in several ways. Preserves give
federal protection to wild areas, but allow some activities not usually permitted in national parks. In
Big Cypress, for example, private landowners keep
their land, cattle graze in some portions, hunting continues, off-road vehicles roam and an airstrip
operates.

The preserve covers about forty percent of the Big
Cypress Swamp, but the government continues to ex-
pand the preserve through purchases and trades. The

entire Big Cypress Swamp covers twenty-four hundred square miles of southwestern Florida. That's an area a little larger than the state of Delaware.

The "Big" in the name refers to the swamp's area, rather than the size of the trees. The "Swamp" in the name is misleading. Only about one-third of the Big Cypress area is cypress swamp. The other two-thirds includes sandy islands covered with slash pine, mixed hardwood hammocks, wet prairies, dry prairies, marshes and estuarine mangrove forests. Dwarf pond cypress trees line the sloughs and edge the wet prairies, forming occasional cypress domes.

The area once had an abundance of towering, hundred-foot-tall bald cypress trees. But few remain. In the 1930s and '40s cypress lumber became valuable enough to make it pay to cut and haul the giants. The building of the Tamiami Trail made the trees accessible. Good pay persuaded men to work under difficult conditions — mosquitoes, hip- or waist-deep water, rocky terrain with booby trap-like solution holes and strength-sapping summer heat and humidity.

When the Everglades is spoken of in its broader sense the Big Cypress Swamp is included. At times of high water the swamp overflows into the Everglades. Otherwise its water moves southwesterly into the Gulf of Mexico.

Leave the Tamiami Trail to experience a bit of the Big Cypress away from the highway. Take Loop Road, which runs west from Forty Mile bend, where the Tamiami Trail turns northwest. Farther on Loop Road turns north and will return you to the Trail.

A few miles along this narrow road stands the

Park Service's Loop Road Interpretative Center. Students from surrounding areas come here to camp and learn about the Everglades and Big Cypress. At the center, a short trail leading through Liguus (pronounced LIG-you-us) Hammock will let you learn about another form of life in the Everglades.

Liguus Hammock

This hammock is named for the colorful tree snails that occur in hammocks throughout South Florida. The only other places they are found are on the Caribbean islands of Cuba and Hispaniola.

As you walk along the trail, you shouldn't have to go too far before finding one of the snails on a tree

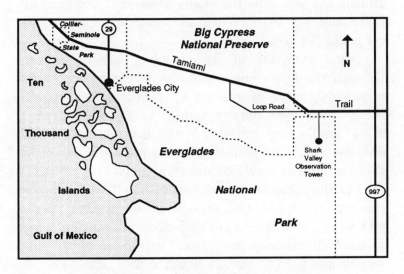

The Everglades — Tamiami Trail Area

trunk. About one and a half inches long, its whorls are banded in stripes, perhaps of patterned brown and tan with a rosy tan tip. Colors in other hammocks range from almost pure white to combinations of yellow, orange, blue and green, as well as the brown and tan bandings. These snails rival birds and butterflies as the most beautiful of creatures found in nature.

Ligs, as they are called, eat lichens that grow on the trunks and limbs of hammock trees. They live only in hammocks, and each hammock has its own variety of snail, or mix of varieties. When the dry season comes, they secrete a substance that seals their shells to the bark of a tree. They remain there in a state of suspended life called **aestivation** until the rain returns. Should you see any snails, do not try to pick them up. If their seals are broken, they will die. During the wet time the snails descend to the ground, mate and lay eggs. When they hatch, young snails return to the trees to live.

Some varieties of liguus have become extinct through the loss of hammocks to development, others because they are of interest to collectors. Greedy collectors have even burned hammocks so that the variety of snails they collected would become extinct. No one else would be able to get that particular type, so their specimens would be more valuable.

Farther back in the hammock you'll discover the remains of an old still, once used for making illegal whiskey. The battered pot and circle of stones around weathered charcoal have been left to illustrate one way people used to make a living in this isolated area.

After the Tamiami Trail opened, lumbermen,

hunters, fisherman, guides and cattlemen came to the Big Cypress and built several small towns. Today they are almost, but not quite, ghost towns. A few rugged outdoor people still endure the heat, humidity and mosquitoes to enjoy the beauty and solitude.

Leave the Interpretative Center and continue along Loop Road. You'll find it is now rough and potholed, but it's passable if taken slowly. The road takes you through wet prairie with pond cypress. Stop to hike into one of the thick stands. Although the trees in a stand may only be about fifteen feet tall, they are perhaps five hundred years old.

The array of bromeliads will impress you. They festoon the little trees in almost unbelievable numbers. Green anoles may also be numerous. Should you spot one of these small lizards he may seem to be doing push-ups while displaying at his throat a red fan which he opens and closes in territorial display. Anoles are sometimes called chameleons because of their ability to change color, but true chameleons are not native to the Americas.

If your eyes are sharp, you may see a green tree frog squatting on a green leaf in the understory. Ivory stripes will mark his sides, golden circles will ring his eyes and golden flecks will speckle his green skin.

You could encounter a box turtle waddling along. As you approach, it will become motionless, drawing in its head and feet. These turtles don't differ much from the box turtles found throughout North America.

On one of my visits to this area, I spotted a clump of pearly white apple snail eggs the size of BB pellets clinging to pickerel weed in the canal alongside the road. Nearby was a heap of empty, round, brown apple snail shells. They were about the size of Ping-Pong balls. These snails are the only food eaten by a distinctive bird — the snail kite, also known as the Everglades kite. The snail kite is another endangered resident of the Glades. Probably less than five hundred remain in Florida.

A shortage of apple snails is one of the reasons the snail kite is endangered. Draining of wetlands and flooding in other areas has reduced the snail population. If water gets too high, it drowns the developing snail in its egg.

The pile of shells I saw, however, was probably left by a limpkin, another snail-eating bird. Limpkins are wading birds who hunt the snails in shallow water and leave piles of shells at the water's edge. Snail kites hunt while flying over the water and take the snails to a tree to feed on them.

A third bird, the boat-tailed grackle, also eats apple snails and hunts at water's edge as do the limpkins. Grackles are blackbirds. They are numerous in South Florida and are found in urban areas as well as the wilderness.

Limpkins and grackles eat other things in addition to snails. But the snail kite's bill is specially adapted, so it eats only snails. It tears off the operculum — a plate that closes and seals the shell — and pulls the snail out.

In addition to a decreased food supply, destruction

of habitat and shooting have contributed to the plight of the kites. They are hawks, and some people think shooting hawks is okay.

Efforts to save the species concentrate on keeping water levels correct for the snails to prosper, preserving kite nesting places, preventing shooting and publicizing the kite's endangered status.

Collier-Seminole State Park

When Loop Road brings you again to the Tamiami Trail, turn left to continue west along the Trail. About sixteen miles west of the Trail's intersection with State Route 29 you'll reach Collier-Seminole State Park. Bordered by the Big Cypress Swamp and the Everglades, this state park offers you an opportunity to take to the water and get a different view of the Everglades.

To explore the park's wilderness preserve from the water, you have two options. A tour boat makes daily narrated trips throughout the year. Or, during the winter season, you can sign up for a ranger or volunteer-led canoe trip. Rental canoes are available. But call ahead (813-394-3397) to find out when the trips are scheduled. If you prefer, you can make the thirteen-and-a-half-mile canoe trip on your own.

If you canoe, you'll paddle through an extensive mangrove swamp. Occasional egrets and herons may look up from their trail-side perches, or take off with a scolding squawk if they feel disturbed by your approach. Green-walled corridors absorb the quiet splash of canoe paddles and the muted voices of canoers. The wilderness embraces you.

At Mud Bay a broad opening in the mangroves gives a more open view of the sky. The bay also marks the turn around for the three-hour guided trips.

Back on land you can see the park's "walking dredge." An adjacent display board explains how road crews used this odd machine to help build the Tamiami Trail. Nearby, you'll also find a replica of a blockhouse used by U.S. troops during the Second Seminole War.

Head for the park's nature trail, either on your own or with a ranger-guided tour. The trail takes you through three distinct ecosystems: a hardwood hammock (compare this hammock with the one you visited on the Gumbo Limbo Trail), a mangrove-buttonwood forest and a salt marsh.

Salt marshes don't impress most visitors. You see an expanse of grasses and rushes dotted with an occasional blossom — the white of a salt marsh aster, the pink of a salt marsh mallow, the lavender-pink of a marsh fleabane or perhaps the scarlet of a southern red lily. Occasionally, you might see a hawk soaring above watching for a marsh rabbit or a snake to eat.

Most of the active life of a salt marsh is hidden among the plants and in the water. But if you understand the function of a salt marsh, you'll gain an appreciation for their importance.

Salt marshes are similar to mangrove areas in nurturing a variety of sea life, especially young shrimp and numerous species of juvenile fish. These youngsters feed on the teeming microscopic life and the barely visible creatures who live on those invisible multitudes. Like mangroves, these marshes also serve as buffers that protect inland areas during storms and filter pollution from fresh water runoff before it reaches the shoreline. This particular salt marsh holds an essential place in the life of the lower edge of the Everglades.

Everglades City

Leaving Collier-Seminole State Park, back track on the Tamiami Trail to State Route 29. Turn right to head south. After about three miles you'll arrive at Everglades City, the western entrance to Everglades National Park. But for now continue driving on State Route 29. You'll cross a bridge and a causeway to reach the island and town of Chokoloskee on the edge of Chokoloskee Bay. The bay lies between the mainland and the Ten Thousand Islands. As you drive you can see a few of the islands across the water.

The road ends on the island, which is actually a shell mound. Shell mounds built by the Calusa Indians are numerous in this part of South Florida. Shellfish were a staple in the diet of these Indians. Some mounds simply grew as the shells were discarded over hundreds of years, but others were built as centers for religious ceremony.

One of the two highest spots in the Ten Thousand Islands, Chokoloskee mound is twenty feet high and covers 135 acres. After the Calusas, Seminoles used the mound and then white fishermen settled there.

Today tourists and sport fisherman occupy the island.

Return to the small town of Everglades City, and stop at the national park visitor center. Board a concession boat here for a tour of a few of the Ten Thousand Islands. These mangrove islands extend in a strip about twenty miles long and five miles wide. They are seemingly uncountable and continually changing in number. Storms destroy some. But wind, waves and washed-in mangrove seedlings build up others.

The mangroves are home to ospreys and cormorants and rare bald eagles. Migrating white pelicans visit Chokoloskee Bay. And the waters around the islands are home to dolphins and manatees.

Bottle-nosed dolphins are small whales. These highly intelligent mammals perform and delight audiences in marine shows around the country. They have also been trained for special duties with the U.S. Navy. The untrained dolphins found in open waters seem to be performing, too, as they follow boats, diving and jumping.

Manatees, also known as sea cows, are on federal and state endangered lists. An estimated fifteen hundred live in Florida. Large, slow-moving mammals, manatees are frequently injured by boat propellers. They are shaped like blimps, with short front flippers and a flat, rounded tail. They may weigh as much as a ton and grow to be fifteen feet long. Manatees are distant relatives of elephants, and their flippers have toenails similar to those of elephants.

Manatees eat only plants, and their only enemies

are people. In the past they were hunted for food. Today it is speeding boats that kill them. During the winter manatees move into canals — especially where power plants discharge warm water — and to springs where water temperatures are constantly warm. To protect them, the State of Florida has designated idle and slow-speed zones for boaters in waters frequented by manatees.

The survival of manatees as a species is doubtful. They reproduce slowly, and, in spite of regulations, boats still kill many manatees.

Your tour boat will probably pass close to an osprey nest. Ospreys are fish-eating birds of prey, also known as fish hawks. You'll notice that the nest, which will probably be in the top of a mangrove tree, is a large collection of sticks and twigs. Ospreys build their nests up to six feet across and line them with grass and weeds. These nests may weigh as much as a half a ton.

Ospreys fish in both fresh- and saltwater. They fly over the water until they spot a fish near the surface. Then, plunging feet first, they grasp the fish with their talons and fly with it to a nearby tree or to their nest to feed. They seem to prefer feeding perched on dead snags.

Ospreys don't like eagles. One reason may be that eagles, who are less skilled at fishing, sometimes harass ospreys, causing them to drop their fish which the eagle then catches.

You'll see double-crested cormorants perched on the posts of channel markers. Almost every post will have its bird. These fish eaters swim on the surface of the water until they spot a fish, then dive and swim after it underwater. Cormorants are able to dive deeply. Like anhingas, their feathers become water-soaked, and you may see them with wings spread to dry after a swim.

You have now seen most of the easily accessible parts of Everglades National Park. But there are still some special places to see in the Big Cypress National Preserve and the Fakahatchee Strand State Preserve.

7

Panther Country

A boardwalk winds among tall cypress trees. Their soaring trunks are unmarred by limbs up to a height of perhaps fifty feet. There a lofty canopy branches out. Water surrounds their trunk bases which spread broadly and irregularly in features called buttresses. Because cypresses grow in wet, unstable muck, the buttressing gives needed support. Reaching out of the water around the bases are knobby projections called knees. They too help to stabilize the tree and possibly serve to take in oxygen for the water-covered roots.

Networks of strangler fig roots entwine many of the big trunks. The figs don't seem to be as successful in killing these giants as they are with the smaller palms. In some places the growth of the cypress has pulled apart the network of fig roots and you can see gaps.

The understory of lower-growing trees includes pond apple, pop ash and red maple. On fallen trees, lush growths of resurrection fern and royal fern reflect in the black swamp water between the floating yellow blossoms of bladderwort, an insect-eating plant. The big leaves and white flowers of the arrowroot and the bright blue flowers of pickerel weed border the water. All around, the light glows green, filtered through the branches overhead.

Except for the presence of the convenient boardwalk, this is the Florida of hundreds of years ago.

Fakahatchee Strand State Preserve

This cypress swamp and boardwalk are located in Fakahatchee Strand State Preserve. You'll find the entrance to this portion of the preserve on the north side of the Tamiami Trail at Big Cypress Bend between Collier-Seminole State Park and State Road 29. Indian Village, a souvenir shop, helps mark the entrance.

In South Florida the term *strand* refers to a long narrow forest of trees growing along a slough. *Fakahatchee* is a Seminole Indian word meaning "River of Vines." There are vines along the preserve's Fakahatchee River, but it is more a river lined with trees.

This preserve lies west of the Big Cypress National Preserve and extends from the edge of the Ten Thousand Islands, at Fakahatchee Bay, north across

Tamiami Trail and on for about twenty miles. The
strand continues beyond the preserve for another five
miles or so to cover a total of some sixty-two thousand
acres.

To see more of the preserve, after leaving the
boardwalk double back to State Road 29 and drive
north to turn onto Janes Memorial Scenic Drive. No
lofty cypress trees line this road. The Fakahatchee
Strand too was logged for its valuable cypress wood.
The small portion along the boardwalk in Fakahatchee and another portion in the Corkscrew Swamp
— which you'll explore shortly — are about all the big
cypresses that remain in the Big Cypress Swamp.

Janes Drive is an unpaved road, rough and in dry
weather dusty. To appreciate the beauty of the strand,
you'll have to park your car and take a wet walk. Stop
first at the ranger headquarters in Copeland (telephone 813-695-4593 to check schedules). This wet
walk must be done with a ranger or other leader with
a compass. It would be easy to become lost in the
pathless swamp.

On your wet walk you'll wade among the young
cypresses that were too small to be logged. Epiphytes
abound in their branches. More kinds of orchids grow
here than anywhere else in North America. Royal
palms grow among the cypress, the only place in the
world where royal palm and cypress mingle.

The water is black from decaying vegetation. Most
of it is knee-to-thigh deep. You can't see the bottom, so
your feet find their way by feeling for unseen roots or
slippery vegetation. A good stout walking stick will
help you to keep your balance.

Water snakes inhabit the area, but you probably won't see any. A few black bears and Florida panthers still live in the area, but visitors seldom catch a glimpse of them. The snakes and animals in this seldom-visited area are reclusive and make themselves scarce when they sense human approach.

Wet shoes and pants legs are a small price to pay to get into this unmarked wilderness. You'll get a feel of connecting with nature that doesn't occur walking with dry feet on a boardwalk.

Many of the plant and animal species in Fakahatchee Strand are rare and endangered, none more so than the Florida panther. No one knows exactly how many of these animals remain, but estimates range from thirty to fifty.

Florida panthers are a subspecies of animals that are called puma, cougar or mountain lion in the western United States, Mexico and Central and South America. The animals of the various subspecies differ in some ways, but they could mate with each other and produce offspring.

You can tell Florida panthers from their relatives by such marks as flecks of white on their shoulders, cowlicks on their backs and crooks in their tails. They are also smaller than their western cousins.

Fakahatchee Strand and the western part of the Big Cypress are considered panther country. Panthers, or similar subspecies, once roamed over much of the United States. But today Florida is the only place any are left east of the Mississippi River.

The Florida Panther National Wildlife Refuge created in 1989 may help save the panthers. The land, thirty thousand acres adjoining the Big Cypress National Preserve, will protect habitat for the panthers as well as six other endangered species, including the bald eagle and wood stork.

Panthers are large cats. Adult females weigh between sixty and one hundred pounds and are about six or seven feet long. Males are larger and can be over one hundred pounds and eight feet long. These cats are not as big as a lion you might see in a zoo, but they are larger than all but the biggest dogs.

Federal and state agencies have formed a committee to try to prevent extinction of the panther, and a captive breeding program has been started. A major cause of panther deaths is the automobile. Many of the animals are killed crossing roads, especially at night. To help prevent such deaths, signs have been posted along the two roads that cross panther country — the north-south State Road 29 and Interstate 75, an east-west toll road also known as Alligator Alley. Some signs warn of stretches where the cats are known to cross. Others say: ONLY 30 REMAIN. Still others are speed limit signs setting the maximum speed at night lower than in the day because panthers move around more at night.

Corkscrew Swamp Sanctuary

From Janes Drive return to State Road 29 and drive north to Immokalee then south and west on State

Road 846 to reach Corkscrew Swamp Sanctuary. Corkscrew got its name from the twisting stream it surrounds. Concerned members of the Audubon Society saved this cypress-filled land from the loggers. A wood stork colony that nested in the cypresses each year aroused the interest of bird lovers. They prevented the big trees from being logged and preserved the rookery. Today, the society continues to maintain the sanctuary.

After entering, follow the path leading through the high ground of a pineland. It takes you to a boardwalk over a wet prairie. As the ground level gradually drops and more water stands for longer times, the prairie gives way to cypress. The cypresses you see at first are the small pond variety, but larger and larger trees are ahead.

If you are exploring in spring, before the walk takes you into the shade of the big trees watch overhead for swallow-tailed kites. These rare hawks spend winters in South America but come to southern Florida to nest in early spring. They have white underparts, deeply forked black tails and black bordered wings. They soar easily, riding the columns of rising hot air known as thermals. Their spread wings let the air take them higher. Then they may tilt and dip lower as if they have spotted food. They eat lizards, snakes and frogs. They also catch insects while flying.

Along the boardwalk, among the large old cypress trees, it is generally quiet. Occasionally a cardinal might call. Perhaps you'll hear a twitter of migrating warblers or the subdued voices of other visitors. But sometimes in spring this is a noisy place, with hundreds of wood stork babies clamoring to be fed as busy parents came winging in to their bulky stick nests. Dozens of nests may be clustered on the top branches of each tree.

If the winter has been wet or too dry the wood storks do not nest. These birds need a concentrated supply of fish to feed their hatchlings. When water levels in the swamp are high, the fish spread out and the storks can't find enough for their babies. The storks seem to be able to judge levels and do not try to raise young when the water isn't right.

Wood storks feed in shallow water, pushing their open bills around underwater. If the bill touches a fish, it snaps shut with split-second timing. It is the stork's unusual manner of feeding that makes the low water level necessary. Most other fish-eating birds rely on sight to find their food.

Wood storks are an endangered species. Much of the swampy spawning ground for fish has been drained to make way for human activities. In the remaining areas water levels are manipulated to suit the desires of people unconcerned about wildlife. Each year there are fewer storks to nest, and when those few don't nest because of inappropriate water levels, the continued existence of the species is jeopardized.

The walkway circles back toward the entrance. Before ending, it crosses a shallow "lettuce lake" covered with rosettes of water lettuce. They look like leaf lettuce.

See if you can spot any alligators sunning themselves among the water lettuce. If you are lucky, maybe you'll see a mother and her young. Some of the baby alligators may be crawling around on their mother's back. Perhaps on a log beside her more babies are clambering over each other. Still others may swim to her and climb up to rest on her snout. Alligators are one of only a few reptiles that show any mothering instinct. If you see young ones, they probably hatched the preceding summer.

Usually around June, possibly later, alligators are building their nests. A gator builds her nest by piling up plants and muck to make a mound high enough to keep the eggs above water. After she lays the eggs, anywhere from twenty to fifty of them, she piles more plants and mud on top. The decaying plants generate heat to incubate the eggs, and the plants and mud insulate them from changes in temperature outside the nest.

The female alligator generally stays near the nest until the young hatch, normally after about sixty-five days. The babies begin grunting before they hatch. If the mother is close by, she will hear them and help by pulling the covering plants off. But even if she doesn't help, the babies can still climb out. When they emerge from the nest they immediately head for water.

Newly hatched gators are about eight or nine inches long. They have orange-yellow stripes, like sunlight through the leaves, which help them hide in the swamp. Many creatures like to eat young alligators. But mother gator stays with them for a year or more, and her presence helps keep would-be diners away.

While they are small, the young continue to make grunting noises. Perhaps that helps the mother keep track of them and to keep the brood, called a pod, together. If one of the little gators gets into trouble, the grunt changes to a cry of distress, and the mother will respond with hisses or lunging at the threatening animal or person. She may even take the little one into her mouth to remove it from danger.

Alligators were listed as an endangered species in 1967. But they have become a success story. With protection their numbers increased, and they have been removed from the list. They are still protected, but in some areas limited, controlled hunting is allowed. Knowing that this animal that once seemed headed for extinction has made a comeback encourages efforts to preserve other endangered wildlife. Let's hope that those other species, especially the wood stork and the Florida panther, fare as well.

Little blue heron

Florida panthers

Upper: white-tailed deer, lower: purple gallinule

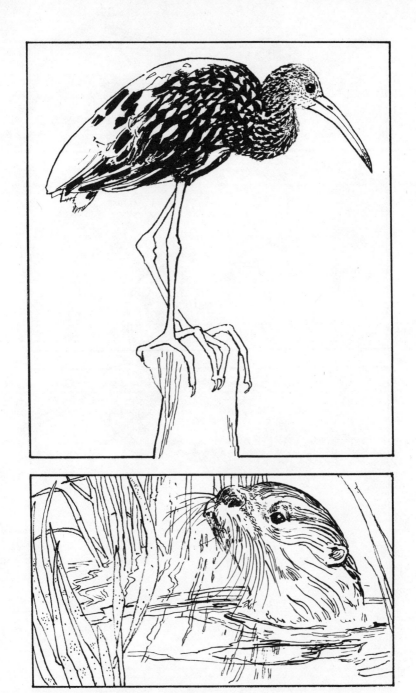

Upper: limpkin, lower: otter

Upper: cormorant, lower: tri-colored heron

Upper: swallow-tailed kite, lower: snail kite

Upper: osprey, lower: eagle

Wood storks

8

Alligator Alley

Travel back across the Glades on Alligator Alley, once a two-lane toll road. Completed in 1969, the road is being widened to become part of Interstate 75.

The American Automobile Association opposed construction of the original road, which was to be named Everglades Parkway. They thought a two-lane road would be unsafe, and they did not like the idea of a toll road. Miami-area boosters also objected to the road. They wanted the Tamiami Trail to be widened and to become part of Interstate 75.

The AAA made fun of the road by calling it Alligator Alley, but the name caught on and has gained official status. Today, the name Alligator Alley is used with pride and affection.

The road runs between Fort Lauderdale and Naples. At its eastern end, the Alley is about 25 miles north of the Trail. But at Naples the two roads meet.

The workers who built Alligator Alley had to contend with the same problems faced by those who built the Tamiami Trail. And the crews constructing the additional interstate lanes also have to face the heat, rainstorms, mosquitoes and snakes. The builders of the Alley and the interstate lanes, however, have been able to take advantage of improved road building know-how and equipment. Using airboats and helicopters to move people and supplies, they took only three years to build the original two lanes.

Engineers designed this second road across the Everglades so that it would provide better water drainage than the Tamiami Trail, but it still obstructs the flow. The new interstate, scheduled for completion in late 1992, is supposed to further improve drainage.

To help protect wildlife, the interstate is fenced in and has a number of animal underpasses. These are intended to allow wildlife to move freely and safely by not having to cross on the road itself. Studies of present animal crossings were used to determine the locations for the underpasses.

The western portion of Alligator Alley runs through the Big Cypress National Preserve. Pond cypress trees line the road. On higher ground slash pines join the cypress. Clusters of epiphytes fill the cypress trees. Many visitors think the clusters are bird nests. Some also think the trees are dead because they drop their leaves in winter and are bare at the time most visitors come to Florida.

Farther east, the road leaves the Big Cypress behind. Saw grass glades, with their accompanying tree
islands, then spread on either side of the road to the
horizon.

As is typical in South Florida, a canal borders the
road. Egrets, herons and an occasional wood stork
wade and fish in the canal. You may also see anhingas
spreading their wings in the trees and turkey and
black vultures soaring overhead.

A little less than two miles east of the Collier-
Broward County line a road on your left leads north to
a Seminole Indian reservation. This road has its canal, too, and a pumping station sits at the intersection
of the two roadside canals. This is a portion of Conser-

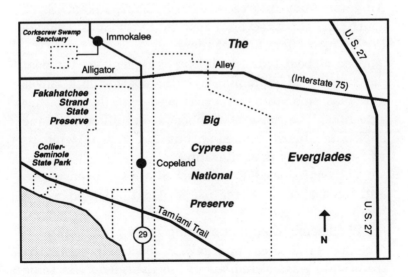

The Everglades — Alligator Alley Area

vation Area 3. Water can be pumped from the canals into the conservation area or from the area back to the canals.

Conservation areas are vast tracts of the Everglades that have been enclosed by levees and surrounded by canals. They enclose 13,370 square miles, or about half of the original Everglades. The conservation areas allow storing water when it is plentiful and releasing it when needed. Conservation area managers do provide public access for hunting, fishing and wildlife viewing. Concessions also provide boat rentals and airboat tours.

Here's your opportunity to ride in an airboat. When Alligator Alley intersects with U.S. 27, take U.S. 27 south for about seven miles to Everglades Holiday Park which offers airboat tours.

The airboat tour I took here is typical. As the boat picks up speed, skimming over the spatter dock leaves and blossoms, the saw grass and cattails on either side blur. The noise of the boat's unmuffled airplane engine is almost deafening, but the rush of wind as you speed along is exhilarating.

The boat slowed as we reached a bit of open water, and we docked at a tree island. On the island was a "Seminole village."

We disembarked and a young Indian man led us to a cluster of chickees and gave a short talk about the traditional ways of Indians in the Everglades. In some of the chickees Indian handicrafts similar to those at the Miccosukee village are displayed for sale.

Back on the water, the boat seemed to be almost flying through the Glades. The driver spotted an alligator as we neared a canal and slowed the boat. A few moorhens with their chicks were paddling around close to the canal bank. "Alligator snacks," the driver called them.

Farther along, a green-backed heron sat on her nest in a pond apple tree on the bank. The boat edged up to almost within touching distance for its passengers. The sitting bird seemed undisturbed, eyeing us without moving.

Except for canoes, airboats are probably the least destructive method of transportation in the Everglades. Because an airboat skims over the vegetation it quickly recovers, unless a route is used repeatedly. Then a trail remains for many years.

Airboats were invented twice. Glenn Curtiss, an American aviation pioneer who liked to hunt in the Everglades, came up with the first airboat around 1920. A pair of frog hunters — frog legs have been on South Florida menus for many years — also developed an airboat around 1933. None of the inventors bothered to patent their idea, and after the 1933 invention other frog hunters copied the concept.

For many years hunters and fisherman were the only airboaters. Today, naturalists and game wardens also use airboats in their work and some people have airboats just for the fun of scooting around the glades.

Everglades National Park permits only park personnel to use airboats.

Back on U.S. 27, which runs north-south through the
eastern Glades, drive north, continuing beyond the
highway's intersection with Alligator Alley. You are
now headed for Lake Okeechobee.

9

Lake Okeechobe

Riding along U.S. 27 you'll see how man has changed the Everglades. This area hardly resembles its original state. The highway, bordered by canals, cuts through the conservation areas. You'll see little wildlife, and the invading Australian pines and melaleuca trees often line the canals.

After about fifteen miles you'll enter the Everglades Agriculture Area. Extensive fields used for farming spread out from either side of the road. Sugar cane is the biggest crop, covering more than four hundred thousand acres, but there are also sod farms growing grass to decorate new housing developments. South Florida's rapid growth creates a big market for lawn sod. In winter, some of the land also finds use for vegetable farming.

The agricultural area begins about twenty-five to thirty miles south of Lake Okeechobee and extends north to curve around both the lake's lower east and west shores. The area takes in more than one thousand square miles, all of which was once a part of the Everglades.

While Lake Okeechobee is a large lake, covering 730 square miles, it's quite shallow, averaging only about twelve feet. The water flowing into the lake first starts its journey a hundred miles to the north, at Turkey Lake near Orlando and Disney World. Creeks, streams, lakes and rivers move the water south. Okeechobee's greatest source of water is a river called the Kissimmee (pronounced ku-SIM-ee). In the past — before man decided to make changes — whenever the southbound flow filled the lake, water spilled out and moved south and southwest to become the Everglades.

When you reach the town of South Bay you have arrived at Lake Okeechobee, but you won't see the lake. A high dike blocks any view of the water. Follow U.S. 27 about seven miles around the lake to the northwest, and stop at John Stretch Park. Here you can climb a stairway to the top of the dike, which a sign identifies as the Herbert Hoover Dike. Water control gates sit in it, and a broad canal — the Rim Canal — leads away from the gates. But you still won't see the lake, only the canal and swamp stretching to the horizon.

Turn back south on the highway for about one-

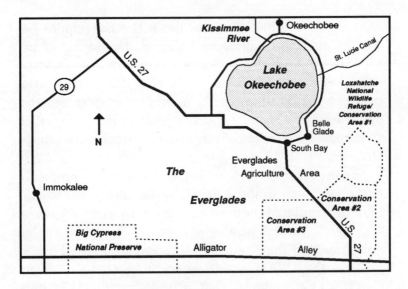

Lake Okechobee Area

fourth of a mile to the Everglades Reclamation State Historical Site. The site is a lock in one of the first drainage canals built in the Everglades. The now-rusting, hand-operated locks raised and lowered boats traveling to and from the lake on the old Miami Canal.

When many early Floridians looked at the Everglades, they did not see something unique in all of nature. They saw swamps that could be drained to produce farmland.

Attempts to manage the Kissimmee River-Lake Okeechobee-Everglades System first began in the

1880s, but in 1905 efforts to drain the Everglades began in earnest. Engineers believed a network of canals leading to the ocean would drain the swamps south of Lake Okeechobee so that the whole area could be turned into farmland. To oversee the operation, the State of Florida created the Everglades Drainage District and, later, an Okeechobee Drainage District.

Soon after drainage began, however, problems arose. A severe drought dried out the peaty muck that had accumulated underwater for hundreds of years. The muck burned whenever a spark ignited it. Lightening started many such fires, some of which burned for months. What the farmers had thought of as "land" was a material that in some countries is harvested and burned as a fuel for heat and cooking.

That wasn't all. In 1926 and again in 1928 hurricanes brought rains that caused devastating floods on the new farms south of the lake. Water collected behind levees that had been built along Lake Okeechobee's shores. Then the levees broke.

After these disasters, engineers turned their attention to flood control instead of drainage. Florida formed the Central and Southern Flood Control District. To replace the old levees, the U.S. Army Corps of Engineers built the Herbert Hoover Dike along eighty-five miles of Lake Okeechobee's shore. The dike was named for the U.S. president who promoted it.

The lower water levels in the Everglades continued to expose the muck to fires, especially during periodic drought years. The fires created a major problem. When the muck burns down to bare rock nothing will grow for many years. Not only do the farmers suffer, but wildlife loses also.

Between 1948 and 1969, engineers still intent on reclaiming the land created a series of canals, water-holding areas (the conservation areas), pumping stations, water control gates and levees or dikes. (There is no difference between dikes and levees. They are both barriers built to separate water from land. *Dike* is an Old English word. We got *levee* from the French.)

These extensive modifications brought about yet another problem. The changes in water patterns caused changes in both vegetation and wildlife. The National Environmental Protection Act of 1969, however, required the Flood Control District to begin considering damage to the environment when making its water management decisions.

A few years later, the Flood Control District changed its name to the South Florida Water Management District. The SFWMD controls the entire Kissimmee River-Lake Okeechobee-Everglades System. Within limits set out by state and federal laws, the SFWMD manages all the water for a 17,930-square-mile area — that's almost as large as the states of Vermont and New Hampshire combined. The district's management decisions affect the lives of about four and a half million people, not to mention the fate of the birds and other wildlife you've been enjoying during your Everglades explorations.

To get a look at Lake Okeechobee, head for the opposite shore. Leaving the historical site, retrace your route back to South Bay. In the town leave U.S. 27 and pick up State Road 80 going east and north to Belle Glade.

The town has a memorial to the more than two thousand victims of the 1928 flood. The memorial sits on the grounds of the Belle Glade Municipal Library, a one-story building on the north side of the highway which, at this point, is the city's Main Street.

Atop a granite pedestal, the memorial depicts the figures of a man and woman with a child between them running for their lives. The woman clutches a baby in her arms. The adults are looking back over their shoulders, each with an arm raised as if to ward off the onrushing water. Their faces show the horror and hopelessness of their situation. Carved into the granite pedestal is a design of swirling waters engulfing several homes. After viewing the memorial you can understand why, following the hurricane, flood control became a priority which continues to this day.

Drive north out of Belle Glade and pick up State Road 715. The road runs along Okeechobee's eastern dike for about ten miles to Pahokee and the Pahokee State Recreation Area. The word *Pahokee* is another form of the Seminole *Pa-Hay-Okee* meaning grassy water. The park is a narrow strip on the lake shore inside the dike. Here you get your first look at the lake.

Lake Okeechobee's light blue waters stretch to the horizon, mirroring the color of the sky. Far out into the lake, grasses wave above the water. The grasses and the water's light color confirm the lake is shallow.

The deeper the water, the darker blue it is.

Continue north, leaving Pahokee on U.S. 441. After about twelve miles you'll reach Port Mayaca where you can make a brief stop at the St. Lucie Canal. The canal runs east from the lake, taking the most direct route to the Atlantic Ocean. One of the first canals built, engineers expected the St. Lucie Canal to divert Lake Okeechobee's entire water flow to the ocean, drying up the entire Everglades. Obviously, it didn't work.

Follow 441 to the lake's north shore and the canals that drain Nubbin Slough and Taylor Creek into the Okeechobee. Dairy farms and cattle ranches are numerous in the area and are a major source of the nitrogen and phosphorus — referred to as *nutrients* — that pollute the lake.

With too much nitrogen and phosphorus, Lake Okeechobee is in serious trouble. Algae thrive on the nutrients and grow rapidly. In limited quantities algae are beneficial as a food for fish and animal life. But an overabundance of algae uses up the water's dissolved oxygen, suffocating the lake's fish and other marine life. When algae growth kills all animal life in a lake, the lake is said to be dead.

The sudden, rapid growth of algae is called a *bloom.* Besides reducing the oxygen supply, blooms can make it impossible for fish to swim in the water. In extreme cases algae can even prevent the passage of boats.

Next stop is the Okee-Tantie Recreation Area (when U.S. 441 turns north, away from the lake, follow State Route 78 around the lakeshore). The

SFWMD operates the recreation area which offers picnic facilities, camping and a marina. During the winter months, fishing enthusiasts from throughout the United States and Canada fill Okee-Tantie, as well as Pahokee and the numerous privately operated "fish camps" that surround the lake.

Okee-Tantie sits on the lakeshore where the Kissimmee River flows into the Okeechobee. The levee, which runs behind Okee-Tantie so it doesn't intervene between the recreation area and the lake, splits at the Kissimmee. It then continues up both banks of the river — or more precisely, the canal that replaces it. The U.S. Army Corps of Engineers *channelized* the river and tagged it Canal 38.

Channelization, which the Corps of Engineers carried out in the 1960s, reduced the meandering hundred-mile river to a fifty-mile ditch. Wetlands, once watered by the river's oxbow bends, became dry land. Other areas that fluctuated between wet and dry with the seasons are now permanently flooded.

Kissimmee River

The Kissimmee River is the main tributary to Lake Okeechobee, so you may want to see more of it. You can't drive along the river since there is no road, but a boat trip up the canal shows some of the effects of channelization — you can rent a boat at the Okee-Tantie marina.

The river's wetlands once supported rich and varied life. Now unproductive *spoil* banks border the deep canal. Spoil is the material dredged up to create the channel. The dry land has become cattle ranches. In the continuously wet areas behind controlling gates, the former varied plant life has been overrun by a few species that choke out fish, leaving no food for the many birds that once inhabited the area or migrated through.

One section is different. Belatedly realizing the errors of channelization, Florida selected a twelve-mile stretch of the river-canal to became an experiment in dechannelization. Never before, anywhere, had this been tried. The dechannelization was successful. The Kissimmee River was returned to its old river bed in this area, and birds and other wildlife are returning as the plant life reverts to its former diversity.

Pleased with the project's outcome, officials have decided to dechannelize the entire Kissimmee River. But the expense of dechannelization — which includes buying up private lands that will be flooded when the river is restored — means it will be quite a few years before the Kissimmee River returns to its natural state.

Unless you have your own boat, you probably won't be able to view the restored stretch of river. The successfully dechannelized section is located more than twenty-five miles upriver from Lake Okeechobee, too far for your rental boat.

Turkey Lake

If you are in the Orlando-Disney World area, complete your Everglades explorations by taking a look at Turkey Lake, the beginning of the system. This small lake, off Turkey Lake Road north of Universal Studios Florida, sits at the edge of Orlando. A city park, with campground and picnic area, lies along a portion of its shore. The Florida Turnpike skirts it on another. The lake gives no indication that it is the headwaters for the Everglades.

Pollution from as far away as Orlando and Disney World has the potential to affect the Everglades. The U.S. Environmental Protection Agency has fined Walt Disney World in the past and has issued warnings about excess nitrogen and phosphorus in the waste water it releases.

Most of the pollutants from Orlando and Disney World do not reach the Kissimmee River. The area's waters flow through creeks, streams and lakes before reaching the river. It is these bodies of water that hold the nutrients. But left unchecked, the pollutants damage the streams and lakes. And eventually the health of any part of the system will affect the whole.

10

Survival of the Everglades

At the dedication of Everglades National Park in 1947 President Harry Truman said, "We have permanently safeguarded an irreplaceable primitive area." Today, the continued existence of that area in anything like its primitive state is in question.

The park was in trouble even as President Truman spoke. Portions of the Everglades had already been drained. Construction of the Tamiami Trail had blocked the natural water flow. And since Truman's dedication of the park, more canals have been dug, more levees built and another road constructed, all causing additional problems in the Kissimmee River-Lake Okeechobee-Everglades System.

The start of construction on a gigantic jetport in

the Big Cypress Swamp in 1970 brought the park's problems to the attention of people around the country. Plans called for the jetport to have runways six miles long. Planes were to land every thirty seconds. A city of one million people was expected to grow up around it. If construction had continued, it would have destroyed the park. But outraged environmentalists from throughout the country were able to put a stop to the plan.

When the United States was young, when the land seemed vast and the population small, little thought was given to preserving the wilderness. Just the opposite. People were interested in "taming" it.

As more and more people spilled across the land, pushing back the frontier, some far-sighted people became concerned. They thought about saving special areas for everyone instead of letting individuals do as they wanted with them. In 1872 such people brought about the establishment of the first national park — Yellowstone.

Before 1900 enough people were interested in preserving wildlife and wilderness areas to start such organizations as the Audubon Society and the Sierra Club. In the years since, membership in these and numerous other environmental groups has grown.

Moves to save the Everglades first started with attempts to preserve Paradise Key in the 1890s and early 1900s. These were the years when the water-flow changes that now threaten the Everglades with disaster were just beginning. But that threat was not recognized by enough concerned people until much later.

Although the jetport idea would have destroyed the Everglades, it did have one positive effect — it made more people aware of the Glades' problems. People became aware of the importance of the Big Cypress Swamp to the Everglades. And as a result the government established the Big Cypress National Preserve.

More recently, awareness has brought about a "Save Our Everglades" program. In August 1983, Florida's then-governor Bob Graham announced the plan. He declared its goal was to make the Everglades of the year 2000 more like the Everglades of the year 1900 than the Everglades of the 1980s. Graham called on federal, state and local agencies to help.

A year later, a number of national environmental organizations formed the Everglades Coalition. These organizations, representing their hundreds of thousands of people throughout the country, made saving the Everglades their goal. And some of Graham's and the coalition's plans have begun to be carried out, but much remains to be done.

One goal of the Save Our Everglades program calls for the restoration of the Kissimmee River. The successful dechannelization of that twelve-mile stretch proves it can be done. The U.S. Army Corps of Engineers did the channelization work. But before they can begin to restore the river, Congress has to approve the project and provide much of the funding. The South Florida Water Management District has authorized studies, using a model and computers, to determine the best method for carrying out the restoration.

The Save Our Everglades plan also proposes saving Lake Okeechobee. Restoring the Kissimmee River will help — the lake receives thirty-six percent of its water and twenty percent of its phosphorous from the river. If the Kissimmee River is allowed to meander once again through its oxbows, excess nutrients will be filtered from the water.

Because the lake's phosphorus content is one of its major problems, the Save Our Everglades program wants to keep phosphorus-rich cattle wastes from reaching Taylor Creek and Nubbin Slough. These tributaries furnish only four percent of the water but a whopping 29 percent of the phosphorus reaching the lake. By 1992 farmers must have fencing to keep cattle from streams that drain into the lake and must put waste treatment systems into use. Additionally, the state and the SFWMD are buying out some farmers to reduce pollution in the area.

Another goal stresses protecting the conservation areas. The problems here involve dealing with high-nutrient agricultural-area runoff and establishing a more natural wet and dry cycle. Efforts to save Lake Okeechobee resulted in increased problems for the conservation areas. Back pumping into the lake of agricultural runoff with its excess nutrients was curtailed. Instead, the amount of this polluted water pumped into the conservation areas was increased. Now these nutrients are changing vegetation in the conservation areas and adversely affecting wildlife.

Conservation Area 1, which receives most of that runoff, is managed as the Arthur R. Marshall Loxahatchee National Wildlife Refuge. That makes the problem especially serious because the refuge is the year-round home for thousands of water birds, the winter home for thousands more and on the migration route of additional thousands.

Polluted water also moves south through canals into Everglades National Park where the increased phosphorus levels have caused changes in the ecosystem.

In 1988 Dexter Lehtinen, U.S. Attorney General for the Southern District of Florida, filed a lawsuit against the Florida Department of Environmental Regulation and the SFWMD. The suit charged the two agencies with failing to enforce existing state laws that protect Everglades National Park and the Arthur R. Marshall Loxahatchee National Wildlife Refuge from polluted water. The suit cited the pollutants contained in the Everglades Agriculture Area drainage water.

To settle the lawsuit, the State of Florida has proposed cleaning up the drainage by creating marshes to receive the polluted water and filter it by natural processes. The proposal, backed by Florida Governor Lawton Chiles, has the approval of both the U.S. Attorney General and the SFWMD.

The plan calls for the marshes to be developed on land in the Everglades Agriculture Area. Farm crops would be removed from the fields and replaced by natural marsh plants such as reeds, cane rushes and grasses. Polluted water from the remaining farmlands would drain into the new marshes, and the plants would absorb the excess nutrients. Dead leaves and plant stems would decay and some of the nutrients would be recycled into algae growth to be consumed by aquatic organisms as part of a natural food web. The marshes would also provide forage for resident and migrating wildlife, especially waterfowl. A little water would be lost to evaporation and transpiration, but the remaining cleaned-up water would be channeled into the Everglades.

Scientists are not sure how much marsh will be needed to provide adequate filtering to enable the runoff water to meet clean-water standards — a preliminary standard by 1997 and a long-term goal by 2002. The state proposes to start with about thirty-five thousand acres. If that proves insufficient, additional land would be acquired.

Farming interests in the agriculture area, however, have not given their approval to the plan. The agribusinesses haven't even conceded that their pollutants are a problem. They also don't want to give up the land necessary to create the marsh, and, because their part of the financing has not yet been determined, they are concerned about what it will cost them.

The cleanup will be expensive — estimates run to $400 million. Although not having acknowledged fault, agriculture has agreed to pay a share. But they want that share to be set at what they consider appropriate.

The general public seems to feel the agricultural industry should pay most, if not all, of the cleanup bill. Many point out that other industries pay for cleaning up water they use before returning it to public waters. Everglades agriculture, however, has not had to do this in the past and doesn't want to accept a major share of the cost now.

The sugar industry, the major agribusiness in the Everglades Agriculture Area, is politically powerful and could stall the cleanup process. To avoid delays, Florida may have to compromise with agriculture. Tests have indicated that the effects of phosphorus pollution are irreversible, which adds a sense of urgency to the need for the cleanup.

To get work on the plan started, and to ensure it continues, the state may have taxpayers living in the SFWMD pick up a portion of the cost. The state may also draw on other readily available sources of financing, including money in Preservation 2000, a fund for buying land for preservation.

The federal government also plans to give added protection to Everglades National Park by enlarging it with the purchase of an area known as the East Everglades. The land lies between the park and the westward expansion of development from the Miami area. The 108,000-acre acquisition will be used to help restore a natural water flow and a natural wet-and-dry cycle to Shark Valley Slough.

The federal and state governments are also buying land to enlarge the Big Cypress National Preserve, the Fakahatchee Strand State Preserve and the Florida Panther National Wildlife Refuge. Each land purchase helps the parks by ensuring the land remains undeveloped.

Another difficult problem yet to be resolved is how to create a more natural cycle of wet and dry throughout the Everglades while balancing the needs of an adjacent urban population. The cities along Florida's southeast coast need continued protection from floods and a water supply ensured against drought.

The Save Our Everglades program also listed preserving endangered wildlife as a specific goal. The program's changes aimed at protecting the Everglades itself are also basic to protecting wildlife. But additional steps are being taken. The State of Florida demanded extra underpasses for Interstate 75 to protect panthers from road kill. Interstate roads are primarily paid for with funds from the federal government, but to get these underpasses Florida agreed to pay for them.

Florida panthers are so perilously close to extinction that the state has implemented a captive-breeding program. A few wild panthers are being captured, and their offspring, born in captivity, will be returned to the wild in areas where they no longer exist or to areas where the breeding panthers were captured.

Although not listed as a Save Our Everglades goal, the exotic plant invasion of the Everglades concerns biologists. Scientists are trying to identify the insects that keep melaleuca trees from becoming a pest in their native Australia as they are in the Glades.

Biologists have released plant-eating insects into the conservation areas to control the unrestrained growth of introduced water-dwelling plants — hyacinths, hydrilla and water lettuce. By using insects that feed only on the problem plants, scientists ensure the number of introduced insects is reduced as the exotic plant population is reduced.

All these Everglades-saving projects and plans involve much time and money. But they are not universally accepted. Some people are simply unconcerned. Others actively oppose them. Many opponents spend time and money furthering plans to make money building in the Everglades.

Former-governor Bob Graham, who went on to become a U.S. Senator, looked at the future of the Everglades in an article he wrote in August 1988 for the Fort Lauderdale, Florida, *Sun-Sentinel.* He pointed out that the natural water flow, the heart of the Everglades system, is the key to the future for all species existing in South Florida, including humans. He added:

> Our responsibility goes beyond geographic boundaries. The Everglades, one of only eight international biospheres, belongs to all people. To lose Lake Okeechobee, to lose the panther, is ultimately to lose every interdependent living creature in the chain.

The coming years hold the answer to the fate of the Everglades. For now, there are only questions. Are enough people concerned about the survival of the Everglades so that private interests can be overridden? Did rescue efforts start soon enough? Is it too late? Can the Everglades be saved?

Glossary

Aestivation - A state of suspended life entered into by some creatures during the dry season. Aestivation is similar to cold-weather hibernation.

Bloom - A sudden rapid growth of algae in a body of water.

Brackish - Water with some salt content, but less than sea water. Brackish water occurs where fresh water streams meet the sea.

Bromeliad - A plant family that includes pineapples. Many bromeliads live as epiphytes in hammock trees.

Canopy - The uppermost level of growth in a hammock or forest.

Channelize - The process in which a meandering

river is dug out and converted to a deep, straight canal. Channelizing is usually done to control flooding and to make navigation easier.

Chickee - Type of thatched roof dwelling built by Seminole Indians.

Conservation Area - A water-holding area in the Everglades enclosed by dikes and surrounded by canals. Conservation areas hold water during wet times to release during dry times.

Detritus - Decomposed plant and animal matter.

Ecosystem - A group of interrelating plants and animals and the place where they live.

Epiphyte - A plant that grows on another plant to raise itself into the air and sunlight. An Epiphyte gets its nutrition from the air and moisture around it, not from the plant on which it lives.

Fronds - The leaves of ferns and palms.

Ground Story - Low growth near the ground in a forest or hammock.

Hammock - An area of higher ground where trees can grow with their roots above water even in the wettest times. This elevation may be only a few inches. The term hammock is used for areas larger than tree islands.

Key - An island. Used in the Everglades to designate higher ground often occupied by a hammock.

Marl - Deposit of dissolved limestone and clay.

Nutrients - Chemicals such as nitrogen and phosphorus which often cause excessive plant growth in bodies of water.

Periphyton - A community of plants, such as algae, and tiny animals forming a spongy, floating mass.

Photosynthesis - The process by which plants manufacture carbohydrates using water from soil or the air and carbon dioxide from the air. Sunlight provides the energy to power the process, which also requires the presence of chlorophyll.

Pneumatophores - Pencil-like projections from the roots of black mangroves. Pneumatophores also occur in some other plants.

Propagule - Reproductive part of a plant. Distinguished from a seed in that it does not experience a dormant period.

Rookery - A resting or breeding and nesting place for birds or mammals.

Scutes - The thick horny scales on an alligator's back.

Slough - A deeper trough in the shallow river that is the Everglades. Sloughs channel water flow.

Solution Hole - A hole formed in the underlying rock of the Everglades. Acidic water from rain and plant decay dissolves the rock, creating a solution hole.

Spoil - Material dredged up in the process of digging out a river channel or a canal.

Strand - A forest growing along a slough.

Terrestrial - Plants that grow in the ground. Also a general term meaning of the earth.

Transpire - Evaporation or giving off of water vapor through the leaves of plants.

Tree Island - A raised bit of land in the Everglades, just sufficiently higher than its surroundings to escape flooding and permit trees to grow.

Understory - The plants — such as shrubs — that grow beneath the taller trees in a hammock or forest.

Index

Save hundreds of dollars on your air travel

Fly There For Less

How to Save Money Flying Worldwide

Bob Martin

Whether frequent or infrequent flyer, business or leisure traveler, you can use the hundreds of concrete, easily followed techniques detailed in this book to consistently obtain the lowest fares on domestic and international flights.

Fly There For Less reveals how the airlines establish and market their fares — and gives you complete, step-by-step, easy-to-follow directions on how to put this information to work cutting the cost of your air travel. You'll discover how to:

- Use lesser-known fares to reap air-travel savings.
- Cut your costs by choosing the right airline.
- Save big with little-known ticket sources.
- Open up low-fare opportunities through frequent-flyer programs, last-minute travel clubs, barter exchanges and air courier firms.
- Uncover and take advantage of circumstances to get low fares.
- Master creative money-saving strategies.

You also get complete contact information — names, addresses and telephone numbers, many toll-free — for airlines as well as the people who can help you save money — including discount ticket brokers, travel clubs, air courier firms and discount travel agencies.

Stop spending more than you need to on air travel

Get *Fly There For Less* today
and put these money-saving techniques to work for you

$16.95, Softcover, 320 pages

If not available in your bookstore

Call toll-free 800-654-0403

Fly There For Less saves you money

"Here is a coherent guide to ferreting out favorable fares...a handy reference for cost-conscious travelers...fascinating."
— *Travel & Leisure*

"*Fly There For Less* guides the air traveler through a maze of air fares...You can save some mega bucks from Martin's creative techniques and strategies."
— *Los Angeles Times*

"An exciting new travel guide called *Fly There For Less* ...can save you a substantial amount of money."
— **Arthur Frommer**

"Author Bob Martin helps air travelers get the lowest fares on domestic and international flights."
— *USA Today*

"An informative new handbook, *Fly There For Less,* can help the harried business traveler who doesn't have unlimited resources."
— *The Philadelphia Inquirer*

"In this easy-to-read book, Martin gives you the details so you can decide which (strategies) will work for you."
— *Seattle Post-Intelligencer*

"Included in this book are more strategies for saving money in the air than anyone ever thought possible. This is a great book for travelers looking for ways to avoid handing the airline industry more than they have to."
— *Going Places*

"*Fly There For Less* details cost-cutting methods that can be used by any international traveler."
— *Toronto Sun*

$16.95, Softcover, 320 pages

If not available in your bookstore

Call toll-free 800-654-0403